Take a Chance on FRIENDSHIPS

A Simplified Guide to Finding

and Developing Friendships

Herbert Sennett, Ph.D.

Sennett, Herbert, Take a Chance on Friendships

©2025 Herbert Sennett, LLC. All rights reserved.

Cover art © 2015 Herbert Sennett, LLC

The chart included is the courtesy of www.fppt.com.

ISBN: 9798991434874 (pb)

You may not reproduce any portion of this document in any form without the publisher's or author's written permission except as permitted by U.S. copyright law.

Disclaimer: This publication is intended for information purposes only. Every effort has been made to ensure this information is as complete and accurate as possible. However, there may be mistakes in typography or content. Any mention of books, articles, and websites must not be understood as an endorsement by or of the author or publisher.

CIF Publications, West Palm Beach, FL

Website: www.herbsennett.com

CONTENTS

INTRODUCTION V
FOUNDATIONS OF FRIENDSHIP 8
BUILDING SOCIAL CONFIDENCE 18
NAVIGATING NEW ARENAS 36
MASTERING CONVERSATION 51
EMBRACING CULTURAL DIVERSITY 59
MANAGING SOCIAL ANXIETY 73
EXISTING FRIENDSHIPS 92
NURTURING FRIENDSHIPS 114
OVERCOMING CHALLENGES 124
DEVELOPING EMOTIONAL INTELLIGENCE 138
TECHNOLOGY AND MINDFULNESS 152
BUILDING INCLUSIVE FRIENDSHIPS 168
PERSONAL GROWTH AND FRIENDSHIPS 180
CONCLUSION 196
ABOUT THE AUTHOR 198

For my friend
J. Scott Gruner

Introduction

Welcome to your transformative journey! This book is not just a guide but a beacon of hope, designed to help you explore the depths of your potential and foster the life you have always dreamed of. In these pages, you will find a wealth of insights, practical tools, and powerful strategies that invite you to confront the obstacles that hold you back and embrace the incredible strength that lies within you.

Sadly, it seems easy to become disconnected from our true selves. We face daily challenges that can leave us feeling defeated, uncertain, and unfulfilled. However, it does not have to be this way because it is true that you can change the things you control.

I hope this book serves as a beacon of hope, providing clarity and guidance as you navigate your personal development journey. Each chapter will reveal a new layer of understanding, encouraging you to explore your thoughts, emotions, and actions more deeply.

You are not alone on this path. Countless individuals have walked similar roads, facing fears, breaking old habits, and stepping into their potential. Their stories, shared here, are a testament to the transformative power of friendship. They have discovered that their willingness to change is the key to unlocking their best selves.

Here, we will share their stories and evidence-based practices that can catalyze your growth. Together, we will build resilience, cultivate self-awareness, and foster a mindset primed for success.

This is not just a book but a practical toolkit for life. You will encounter exercises designed to challenge you and prompt reflection on your beliefs and behaviors. As you engage with the material, you are encouraged to embrace vulnerability, knowing that each step you take is significant, no matter how small. You are capable of incredible change. With every page you turn, you will be one step closer to realizing your dreams.

I have written this book as if it were your personal letter. Throughout my life, my friendships have deeply enriched me in more ways than you can imagine. For example, many years ago, I met a man sitting beside me in our seminary classroom. He introduced himself to me.

I am sure neither of us realized that we would

still be good friends forty years later despite the more than 1,000 miles between us. This is why this book is dedicated to him and his friendship with me.

Foundations of Friendship

Friendship is truly one of the most fundamental aspects of life. It is deeply interwoven into the fabric of our society and shapes our individual experiences. To value the friendships in our lives, it is essential to explore their psychological roots, understand their evolutionary roles, and recognize the incredible personal growth they encourage.

The Psychology of Friendship

Throughout history, friendships have been pivotal in human survival and societal advancement. In early tribal societies, for instance, strong bonds among individuals were fundamental in establishing alliances.

These alliances facilitated the sharing of resources and provided mutual protection, crucial for survival in challenging environments. Anthropological evidence suggests that groups with strong interpersonal connections were better equipped to face hardships, as these relationships fostered a sense of community vital for collective resilience. (Dunbar, 1998).

The importance of friendship extends beyond mere survival; it fosters social cohesion within communities. Social cohesion, the willingness of individuals within a society to cooperate to survive and prosper, is deeply rooted in the relationships they cultivate.

For example, research indicates that cohesive groups form networks that allow more effective communication and collective problem-solving (Berkman et al., 2000). This dynamic enables communities to endure and thrive through shared efforts and collaboration.

On a psychological level, friendships satisfy profound human needs. According to Maslow's hierarchy of needs, the fourth level encompasses the need for belonging, which is fundamental for psychological well-being (Maslow, 1943). Friendships provide validation and emotional support and contribute significantly to self-identity.

This sense of belonging nurtures mental health and enables individuals to navigate life's complexities more effectively. Moreover, social identity theory posits that individuals derive part of their self-worth from their connections with friends. Such relationships reinforce a person's social identity within their community, fostering a sense of belonging and acceptance (Tajfel & Turner, 1986).

Friendships also play a significant role in personal development. Engaging with friends exposes individuals to diverse perspectives and ideas, nurturing self-discovery and growth. For instance, through interactions with friends, individuals engage in social learning by observing and imitating the behaviors of their peers.

This process enhances their understanding of diverse viewpoints and experiences, promoting personal growth and a more comprehensive worldview. Research has shown that positive friendships can also lead to increased self-esteem and greater life satisfaction (Reis & Shaver, 1988).

However, the implications of lacking meaningful friendships can be detrimental. Social isolation and loneliness correlate with heightened stress levels, leading to various mental health challenges. A lack of social connections has been associated with increased risks for depression, anxiety, and other psychological disorders (Cacioppo & Cacioppo, 2014).

Extensive studies indicate that individuals with fewer social connections face a higher risk of physical health issues, underscoring the notion that friendships are beneficial for mental well-being and crucial to overall health and well-being.

Friendships are integral to the human experience, providing essential support for survival, cohesion, and personal growth. Whether through emotional validation or by offering diverse perspectives, the positive impact of friendships cannot be overstated. Therefore, cultivating meaningful relationships should be a priority for individuals seeking to enhance their quality of life.

Role of Emotional Intelligence

Emotional intelligence (EI) plays a pivotal role in forming and maintaining strong friendships. EI enables individuals to navigate the complex landscape of interpersonal relationships and is composed of several essential components such as self-awareness, empathy, emotional regulation, and effective social skills.

Research indicates that individuals with high levels of EI are better equipped to foster meaningful connections, as they can accurately perceive and respond to their own emotions and those of others (Mayer, Salovey, & Caruso, 2008).

Self-awareness refers to recognizing and understanding one's emotions and thoughts. This understanding allows individuals to manage their emotional responses effectively, a skill that is crucial in the context of friendship. When conflicts arise, for instance, a self-aware individual might recognize anger or disappointment and choose to respond constructively rather than impulsively.

Emotional regulation—another key component of EI—allows individuals to adapt their emotional responses to various situations, fostering an environment where conflicts can be resolved amicably (Goleman, 1995). For example, consider two friends who disagree. A friend with high EI may pause to reflect on their emotional state before responding, thus avoiding escalation. They might articulate their feelings using "I" statements, such as, "I felt hurt when you did not invite me," instead of casting blame. **This approach clarifies their feelings and opens the door for a more productive dialogue**.

Empathy, the capacity to understand and share the feelings of others, is a fundamental building block of strong friendships. When individuals practice empathy-driven interactions, they create a supportive environment conducive to emotional connection (Rogers, 1961). Research has shown that empathetic individuals are more likely to engage in prosocial behavior, strengthening their relationships (Batson et al., 2002).

Empathy can transform how individuals

respond to each other's experiences in the context of friendship. For instance, when friends share their struggles, an empathetic response might involve active listening and validating their feelings rather than offering unsolicited advice. This creates a safe space where both friends can express themselves freely, deepening their bond.

To develop emotional intelligence, individuals can implement several practical strategies. Mindfulness practices, such as meditation, encourage self-reflection and can significantly enhance self-awareness (Kabat-Zinn, 1990). By regularly engaging in mindfulness, individuals learn to observe their thoughts and emotions without judgment, fostering an acceptance that is crucial for

Conversely, low emotional intelligence can present significant challenges in friendships. Individuals with lower EI may struggle to articulate their emotions, leading to frustration and misunderstandings. This inability to navigate the emotional landscape complicates communication and creates barriers to developing deep, meaningful connections.

An example would be a friend who struggles to express their feelings. They may withdraw during tough times, leaving their companion isolated and confused. Unfortunately, this may ultimately jeopardize the friendship. So, how do we prevent this from happening?

Emotional intelligence is crucial for fostering healthy and fulfilling friendships. Individuals can significantly enhance their relationships by developing EI through mindfulness, journaling, and active listening. Therefore, fostering emotional intelligence is not just a personal development task. It is an investment in the science of social connections and the future of one's friendships.

Extensive research links social connections to enhanced well-being. The Harvard Study of Adult Development, one of the longest-running studies of adult life, underscores that thriving relationships are a cornerstone of life satisfaction. The release of oxytocin and dopamine during positive social interactions engenders feelings of happiness and security, demonstrating the biological basis for friendship's role in promoting mental health.

The role of friendships often extends beyond mere enjoyment. Research has shown that strong social ties are associated with a longer lifespan. Observations of "blue zones," areas where people live substantially longer, indicate that social integration is crucial in maintaining health and vitality into old age. Furthermore, robust friendships can reduce the risk of chronic diseases, underscoring the profound connection between social connections and physical well-being.

The psychological benefits of friendships are equally compelling. Friendships are a buffer against stress, providing coping mechanisms that enhance overall life satisfaction. Individuals with supportive friends often report higher happiness levels, feeling more fulfilled, and possessing greater resilience in facing challenges.

Conversely, weak, or negative social connections can harm mental health. Insufficient or toxic friendships may lead to an increased risk of depression and a sense of social isolation, which can exacerbate feelings of loneliness and despair.

Understanding the foundations of friendship reveals its indispensable role in human life. The interplay between psychological fulfillment, emotional intelligence, and social connection profoundly influences personal development and well-being.

Readers are encouraged to reflect on their friendships and consider the steps they can take to nurture these vital relationships in today's world. Each person has the power to cultivate meaningful connections that can enrich their life experience—an endeavor worth pursuing for everyone.

References

Batson, C. D., Early, S., & Salvarani, G. (2002). "Perspective-taking: Reducing Prejudice and Discrimination." *Journal of Personality and Social*

Psychology, 82(1), 100–115.

Berkman, L. F., Glass, T., Brissette, I., & Seeman, T. E. (2000). "From social integration to health: Durkheim in the new millennium." *Social Science & Medicine*, 51(6), 843–857.

Cacioppo, J. T., & Cacioppo, S. (2014). "Social Relationships and Health: The Toxic Effects of Perceived Social Isolation." *Social and Personality Psychology Compass*, 8(2), 58-72.

Dunbar, R. I. M. (1998). *Grooming, Gossip, and the Evolution of Language.* Harvard University Press.

Goleman, D. (1995). Emotional Intelligence: Why It Can Matter More Than IQ. Bantam Books.

Kabat-Zinn, J. (1990). Full Catastrophe Living: Using the Wisdom of Your Body and Mind to Face Stress, Pain, and Illness. Delacorte Press.

Maslow, A. H. (1943). "A Theory of Human Motivation." *Psychological Review*, 50(4), 370–396.

Mayer, J. D., Salovey, P., & Caruso, D. R. (2008). "Emotional Intelligence: A New Ability or Eclectic Trait?" *American Psychologist.*" 63 (6), 503–517.

Reis, H. T., & Shaver, P. (1988). "Intimacy as an Interpersonal Process." In S. W. Duck (Ed.), *Handbook of Personal Relationships: Theory, Research, and Interventions* (pp. 367-389). Wiley.

Rogers, C. R. (1961). On Becoming a Person: A Therapist's View of Psychotherapy. Houghton Mifflin.

Tajfel, H., & Turner, J. C. (1986). "The Social Identity Theory of Intergroup Behavior." In S. Worchel & W. G. Austin (Eds.), *Psychology of Intergroup Relations*.

Building Social Confidence

Many individuals grapple with social anxiety, often feeling overwhelmed in social settings because of our hectic world. Building social confidence is not merely about developing outgoing traits; it encompasses a deeper understanding of oneself and one's surroundings. One effective approach to fostering this confidence is practicing mindfulness.

Start with Yourself

Many individuals struggle with social insecurities, often feeling overwhelmed in situations that require connection and communication. One of the most effective strategies to combat these feelings is mindfulness. Mindfulness cultivates a sense of inner peace and empowers individuals to manage anxiety, especially in social contexts.

Mindfulness is the practice of paying attention to the present moment without judgment. This practice has gained recognition for its numerous benefits, particularly in promoting confidence and alleviating anxiety. When anxiety strikes during social interactions, individuals often find themselves caught in a whirlwind of negative thoughts and self-doubt.

Mindfulness helps anchor the mind, allowing individuals to focus on their breath, which is a stable point of reference. This shift in focus can significantly diminish feelings of anxiety, making social situations feel more manageable.

For instance, consider the body scan meditation, a simple yet powerful mindfulness technique. In this exercise, individuals are guided to focus on different parts of their body, noticing any sensations without attaching labels of good or bad.

By cultivating a deeper awareness of physical reactions, individuals can begin to understand how their bodies respond to various social scenarios. This, in turn, leads to a better understanding of their emotions and reactions, creating an opportunity for growth and empowerment.

Developing Mindfulness

Establishing a mindfulness practice unlocks opportunities for self-acceptance and personal growth. One effective method is to guide readers through mindfulness exercises that can be integrated into their daily lives.

1. Guided Visualization: Encourage readers to imagine successful interactions in their minds. Visualization can enhance self-confidence by allowing individuals to mentally rehearse positive outcomes, setting a powerful framework for real-life situations.

2. Progressive Muscle Relaxation: This technique involves systematically tensing and relaxing each muscle group. It teaches individuals to recognize the physical signs of tension and anxiety and how to release them.

These exercises can significantly help individuals prepare themselves for social engagement, transforming their perspective on interactions.

Long-term Benefits of Mindfulness Practice

Engaging in regular mindfulness practices yields numerous long-term benefits beyond immediate anxiety relief. Research increasingly shows that sustained mindfulness can lead to a comprehensive reduction in anxiety levels, fostering a deeper emotional connection with others.

Additionally, regular mindfulness practice

enhances self-awareness, enabling individuals to better understand their emotions and develop empathy toward others. These attributes are crucial for building and maintaining rich, meaningful relationships. When cultivated through mindfulness, social confidence leads not only to personal growth but also to a transformation in how one relates to others.

Tips for Daily Implementation

Incorporating mindfulness into everyday life does not have to be daunting or time-consuming. Here are a few simple yet effective methods:

1. Mindful Walking: Take time to walk mindfully, focusing on the sensations of your feet touching the ground, the sounds around you, and the rhythm of your breath.

2. Attentive Listening: During conversations, practice giving the speaker your undivided attention. Acknowledge their words and emotions without planning your response while they speak.

Setting aside just a few minutes for daily meditation can lead to transformative shifts in perspective, fostering a more calm and composed approach to social situations.

Daily Exercises for

Growth

In personal development, cultivating a growth mindset is essential for individuals seeking to enhance their potential and navigate life's challenges with resilience and optimism. Engaging in specific exercises can significantly aid in this transformative journey. Below are some of the most common exercises that individuals can undertake to grow their mindset:

1. Journaling for Reflection: Individuals can set aside time daily to reflect on their thoughts, experiences, and emotions. This practice fosters self-awareness and encourages individuals to identify areas for growth and celebrate their progress. Reflective journaling serves as a reminder of the lessons learned through challenges.

2. Setting SMART Goals: By employing the SMART criteria (Specific, Measurable, Achievable, Relevant, Time-bound), individuals can create clear, structured goals that motivate them to push their boundaries. This exercise helps break down larger objectives into manageable steps, fostering a sense of accomplishment.

3. Affirmations: Positive affirmations can have a profound influence on one's mindset. By repeating empowering statements, individuals can combat self-doubt and build confidence. This exercise enables individuals to reframe negative thoughts and instill confidence in their capabilities.

4. Embracing Challenges: It is vital to encourage individuals to step outside their comfort zones. Whether trying a new activity, tackling a difficult project, or learning a new skill, facing challenges head-on fosters resilience and reinforces the belief that effort leads to improvement.

5. Practicing Gratitude: Keeping a gratitude journal where one writes down things they are thankful for each day can shift one's focus from scarcity to abundance. This exercise fosters a positive outlook and helps individuals appreciate their journey, regardless of the circumstances.

6. Mindfulness and Meditation: Regular mindfulness or meditation practice can enhance emotional regulation, reduce stress, and promote a sense of peace. These practices enable individuals to observe their thoughts non-judgmentally, aiding in developing a balanced and growth-oriented mindset.

7. Seeking Feedback: Encouraging individuals to seek feedback from peers, mentors, or coaches can provide valuable insights into their areas of strength and opportunities for growth. This openness to feedback fosters a culture of continuous learning and improvement.

8. Visualizing Success: Visualization techniques involve imagining oneself achieving specific goals. By vividly picturing success, individuals can better mentally and emotionally prepare themselves, reinforcing their belief in their ability to attain their objectives.

When practiced consistently, these exercises can lead to profound shifts in one's mindset, empowering individuals to embrace opportunities, overcome obstacles, and achieve their fullest potential.

It is essential to remember that every attempt at social engagement, no matter how small, is a step toward building confidence. Celebrate these moments as they contribute to a stronger, more resilient you.

Mindfulness offers a pathway to facing and overcoming social insecurities. Through awareness, acceptance, and practice, individuals can cultivate profound confidence from the inside out, leading to richer, more fulfilling relationships. The journey toward social confidence may be gradual, but you draw closer to the authentic you with each mindful step.

Tracking Progress

Individuals are encouraged to document their experiences and track their progress and improvements to foster motivation. Journaling offers a structured opportunity for self-reflection, allowing individuals to articulate their thoughts and feelings about their daily experiences. By putting pen to paper, they can explore their social interactions, identifying the moments that brought them joy or challenged them, thus fostering a deeper understanding of their behaviors and emotions. This writing process becomes an invaluable tool for personal growth, creating space for clarity and insight.

Another significant aspect of journaling is the setting of personal goals. Individuals can outline their aspirations, breaking them down into actionable steps. This practice helps them visualize their path and encourages accountability; by documenting their goals, they are more likely to commit to them.

Setting intentions fuels motivation by transforming abstract desires into tangible milestones, making the journey achievable. As they write about their objectives, they develop a stronger connection to their aspirations, inspiring them to move forward confidently.

Monitoring progress is essential for reinforcing the habits that lead to success. As individuals reflect on their journey through journaling, they can celebrate their achievements, no matter how small they may seem.

This recognition of progress serves as a motivational boost, reminding them of their capabilities and the efforts they have made thus far. By consistently evaluating their growth, individuals create a positive feedback loop that nurtures resilience and encourages them to maintain the habits that support their personal development. Embracing this practice can lead to a richer, more fulfilling life as individuals continue to evolve and strive toward their goals.

Turning "No" into a Learning Opportunity

Rejection is commonly regarded as a negative experience but can be reframed as a positive force in an individual's journey toward personal growth. By shifting their perspective, one can recognize that rejection is not an end but a stepping stone to greater resilience and self-discovery.

For many, the initial sting of rejection can feel like a blow to their self-worth, yet when approached with an open mind, it serves as a valuable feedback mechanism. This understanding enables individuals to distinguish their identity from rejection, thereby fostering a healthier mindset that accepts life's challenges.

Additionally, viewing rejection through a lens of opportunity can lead to significant introspection and improvement. Rather than spiraling into self-doubt, individuals are encouraged to analyze the reasons behind the rejection.

This process of reflection can illuminate personal strengths and weaknesses, enabling them to harness their experiences for future endeavors. Acknowledging that rejection is often not a personal affront but a contextual challenge can empower individuals to refine their skills, expand their capabilities, and become more resilient.

Ultimately, the experience of rejection can lead to profound personal development. Individuals can transform what initially feels like a setback into a powerful catalyst for change by cultivating resilience and adopting a growth mindset. With each experience of rejection, they become more adept at navigating life's complexities and more confident in their path forward. Embracing rejection as an essential aspect of the journey leads to important life lessons and paves the way for future successes.

Handling Rejection Gracefully

Maintaining composure in the face of rejection is crucial for developing emotional resilience, and individuals can employ several practical strategies. One effective approach is practicing gratitude. When individuals take the time to reflect on what they are thankful for—whether that be supportive relationships, personal achievements, or simply the lessons learned—they can cultivate a more positive mindset.

This gratitude practice shifts the focus away from feelings of disappointment. It helps to reinforce the idea that rejection is just a part of the broader journey toward personal growth and fulfillment.

Another vital strategy involves engaging in positive self-talk. When faced with setbacks, individuals often become their own harshest critics, dwelling on negative thoughts that can hinder progress.

By consciously reframing their thoughts and replacing self-doubt with affirmations of personal strength and capability, individuals can enhance their ability to view failures as valuable learning opportunities. This mindset encourages them to view challenges as stepping stones rather than obstacles, fostering resilience and persistence essential for long-term success.

Furthermore, seeking constructive criticism can be a powerful tool for growth and understanding in social contexts. Rather than shying away from feedback, individuals seeking constructive opinions from trusted peers or mentors can gain insights that inform their personal development.

This openness empowers them to improve and helps mitigate the sting of rejection. By viewing such experiences as opportunities for learning and growth, individuals strengthen their emotional resilience and develop meaningful connections with others, ultimately leading to a richer, more fulfilling life.

Techniques for Building Resilience

Developing a growth mindset (the belief that abilities and intelligence can be developed through effort and learning) is crucial in recognizing rejection as an integral and natural component of human interactions. When individuals adopt this perspective, they begin to see rejection not as a personal failing but an opportunity for growth and understanding.

Rejection often triggers a wave of negative emotions, leading to self-doubt and withdrawal. However, by reflecting on past experiences with rejection, individuals can uncover patterns in their responses and interactions. For instance, someone who consistently avoids social situations due to a fear of rejection may benefit from analyzing their past rejections.

Were there common themes? Did certain situations feel more overwhelming than others? By identifying these patterns, one can develop strategies to approach future interactions with greater resilience and a more open heart.

Furthermore, surrounding oneself with a supportive social network is vital. Friends and family who foster understanding and encouragement create an environment where individuals feel safe to express their vulnerabilities. Engaging with like-minded individuals who share similar experiences can also provide a sense of solidarity. Supportive social dynamics help reinforce the notion that everyone encounters rejection and that it is a universal experience.

To cultivate a healthier relationship with social uncertainties, gradually confronting the fear of rejection through specific activities can be transformative. Volunteering for roles that inherently carry risks of rejection, such as public speaking or performing arts, pushes one beyond one's comfort zone. Such experiences teach valuable lessons about resilience and demonstrate that rejection does not define one's worth.

Participation in clubs or groups that encourage the exploration of new interests also builds confidence. It could be a local improv group or taking a class in a new hobby; these activities allow individuals to engage with others in a low-stakes environment, where the risk of rejection is present but framed within the context of shared learning and enjoyment.

Embracing rejection as a teacher rather than an enemy can lead to profound transformation. By developing a growth mindset, reflecting on past experiences, surrounding oneself with a supportive community, and gradually facing fears, anyone can learn to navigate the complex landscape of social interactions with greater resilience. **Rejection is not the end; it is merely a part of your journey toward personal development**.

Success Stories

Social anxiety can often feel like an insurmountable barrier, isolating individuals from the connections that enrich our lives. However, it is essential to understand that many people have successfully navigated this challenge, finding solace and strength through mindfulness and practice. Sharing these transformative experiences inspires and provides practical tools for those currently on a similar journey.

Real-Life Anecdotes

Consider the story of Sarah, a young professional overwhelmed in social settings. Sarah's journey began when she discovered mindfulness meditation, which she integrated into her daily routine. Set against a bustling corporate world backdrop, she learned to focus on her breath, quieting her mind before entering challenging social scenarios. Over time, this practice enabled her to reframe her anxiety; she began viewing social interactions as opportunities for connection rather than potential pitfalls.

Another powerful example is the experience of Jack, a college student who grappled with severe social anxiety. Jack confronted his fears by engaging in small group discussions centered around topics he was passionate about. Through his commitment to these mindful practices, he gained confidence and forged lasting friendships. Jack frequently notes that his quiet resilience and practice of active listening have transformed his social experiences—allowing him to see the beauty in vulnerability.

Public Figures and Their Struggles

Even notable public figures have faced similar challenges. For instance, actress Emma Stone has openly discussed her battle with anxiety since childhood. Stone utilized mindfulness techniques and cognitive behavioral approaches to cope, noting how these tools allowed her to navigate the pressures of Hollywood. Her story serves as a beacon of hope for anyone feeling alone in their experiences.

Similarly, renowned author Mark Twain dealt with social anxiety throughout his life. Twain's humor and wisdom often reflected his inner struggles, giving readers a relatable perspective. By sharing these stories, we see that social anxiety is more common than one might think—even among those we hold up as beacons of success.

The Power of Mindful Practices

Building social confidence through mindful practices helps individuals regulate their emotions and fosters deeper connections with others. Mindfulness teaches us to be present in the moment, enabling us to listen actively and respond thoughtfully during conversations. This practice cultivates empathy and understanding, key ingredients for any meaningful relationship.

Engagement in social situations—whether through group classes, book clubs, or community events—can amplify these skills. By surrounding ourselves with supportive atmospheres, we can practice combining mindfulness with social interaction, slowly transforming anxiety from a debilitating experience into an empowering journey.

Conclusion

Building social confidence is a crucial journey for individuals seeking to navigate the complexities of social interactions with greater ease and confidence. Through a deep understanding of oneself and the practice of mindfulness, individuals can significantly alleviate feelings of social anxiety. The comprehensive exploration of mindfulness techniques, such as guided visualization and progressive muscle relaxation, equips individuals with practical tools for managing anxiety and fostering self-acceptance.

Incorporating simple daily practices, such as mindful walking and attentive listening, into one's routine can facilitate a gradual transformation in social confidence. This chapter outlines how consistent mindfulness engagement can yield long-term benefits, including enhanced self-awareness, improved emotional regulation, and the cultivation of empathy.

The stories of individuals like Sarah and Jack are powerful reminders that overcoming social anxiety is attainable and that authentic experiences and supportive relationships frame the path to greater confidence. By consistently applying the practices shared in this chapter, individuals can empower themselves to engage more fully in their social lives, turning fear into opportunity and isolation into connection.

Ultimately, the insights presented here highlight that the journey toward social confidence is not merely about external engagement—it is an invitation to cultivate an enriched inner life that translates to genuine interactions with others. Through patience, practice, and mindful awareness, the authentic self can emerge, ready to embrace the connections that add meaning and joy to life.

References

Brown, B. (2012). Daring Greatly: How the

Courage to Be Vulnerable Transforms the Way We Live, Love, Parent, and Lead. Gotham Books.

Brown, B. (2010). The Gifts of Imperfection: Let Go of Who You Think You're Supposed to Be and Embrace Who You Are. Hazelden Publishing.

Dweck, C. S. (2006). Mindset: The New Psychology of Success. Random House.

Kabat-Zinn, J. (2013). Full Catastrophe Living: Using the Wisdom of Your Body and Mind to Face Stress, Pain, and Illness. Bantam.

Goleman, D. (1995). Emotional Intelligence: Why It Can Matter More Than IQ. Bantam Books.

Myers, D. G. (2014). *Social Psychology*. McGraw-Hill.

Neff, K. (2011). Self-Compassion: The Proven Power of Being Kind to Yourself. HarperCollins.

Siegel, D. J. (2010). The Mindful Therapist: A Clinician's Guide to Mindsight and Neural Integration. W.W. Norton & Company.

Stone, E. (2015). The Truth About Anxiety and Me: A Candid Conversation. Thrive Global.

Twain, M. (2007). *The Autobiography of Mark Twain.* University of California Press.

Navigating New Arenas

Stepping into a new city or embarking on a fresh career path can be both exhilarating and intimidating. For many, it is a time filled with questions and uncertainties. How will I meet new people? Where do I begin? The good news is that building meaningful connections in these new environments is possible and an enriching experience that can transform your life.

On a personal note, my parents had to move to another state during my junior year of college. Since my sister was entering her first year of college, I knew my dad could not afford to support two children in two states, hundreds of miles apart. So, I decided to transfer to a college near my parents' new home.

If you are familiar with the college experience, you know that transferring to colleges at the beginning of your senior year is not advisable. That meant I had to spend another year in college to complete my degree. However, I did it anyway to help my parents. As a result,

I made numerous new friends. One was a young lady who later agreed to be my wife. At the time of writing, we are still married.

This chapter will explore the essential steps to navigate the often complex landscape of making friends in unfamiliar settings. The journey of forging friendships begins with your mindset. Viewing this new chapter as an opportunity for growth will, hopefully, allow you to embrace the unknown with enthusiasm rather than apprehension. With an open heart and a willingness to connect, you will find that each new face you encounter is an opportunity to forge a relationship that could enrich your life.

We will discuss practical tips for establishing a social base, including joining local clubs or hobby groups that align with your interests and getting involved in community events that cater to like-minded individuals. Additionally, we will explore how digital tools and resources can facilitate your integration into a new social landscape, making the daunting process of meeting new people more manageable.

Isolation can often creep in when relocating, but we will also consider effective strategies to combat feelings of loneliness. Connecting with old friends and setting manageable social goals, you can maintain a sense of belonging while navigating your new surroundings.

Furthermore, we will examine the art of

attraction—how your body language, attitude, and conversational skills make you approachable. You will learn techniques that empower you to easily break the ice, ensuring you develop meaningful connections from the outset.

As we transition to the professional realm, we will highlight the importance of networking as a key skill, emphasizing strategies for authentic engagement. You will learn how to establish a diverse network that opens doors to new opportunities and provides a supportive community as you navigate your career development.

By the end of this chapter, you will be equipped with the knowledge and confidence to transform the often-overwhelming task of making new friends into a delightful and rewarding experience. Embrace the challenges, cherish the moments of connection, and look forward to lifelong friendships in this new arena. Let us travel together!

Making Friends in a New City or Job

The challenge of building a new social network may seem overwhelming initially, but with the right mindset and strategies, it is entirely feasible to create meaningful connections. The journey of making friends is as much about embracing a fresh perspective as it is about employing effective approaches. By adopting a "fresh start" mentality, individuals can view new environments as fertile grounds for potential friendships, where every unfamiliar face could represent an opportunity waiting to blossom.

Steps for Establishing a Social Base

Building a vibrant social circle starts with proactive engagement in the community. Local clubs, hobby groups, and social classes present excellent opportunities to meet people with shared interests.

For instance, if you are passionate about photography, joining a local photography club can provide friendships and collaborative projects. Research indicates that shared activities can enhance social bonds. Murray and Manzo (2015) found that engaging in shared interests fosters deeper connections and greater personal satisfaction.

Community events and meetups offer another effective platform for meeting diverse individuals. These gatherings enhance social skills and cultivate a sense of belonging within the community.

Volunteering is a meaningful way to connect with like-minded individuals. It promotes shared values and experiences that can significantly strengthen bonds among participants. According to a study by Clary et al. (1998), volunteering can enhance social integration by providing a network of support that contributes to overall well-being.

Local Resources in Social Integration

Navigating a new social environment can be a daunting task, especially for those who find themselves in unfamiliar territory. However, local resources are crucial in easing this transition, particularly in today's digital age. Engaging with social media groups or online forums dedicated to newcomers can provide valuable insights and recommendations for local activities.

For example, platforms such as Facebook often host groups tailored to specific regions or interests, where individuals can share experiences, suggest events, and offer advice to one another. This sense of community can be instrumental in helping newcomers feel more connected and informed about their surroundings.

Moreover, websites like Meetup.com are excellent platforms for individuals to explore interest-based groups and events that align with their hobbies and preferences. Whether someone is passionate about hiking, book clubs, or cooking classes, Meetup enables users to search for gatherings in their local area, fostering opportunities to meet like-minded people. These events often encourage personal growth and the exploration of new interests in a supportive environment.

In addition to social media and event platforms, applications are emerging as invaluable tools for newcomers seeking to integrate into their new communities. Many apps are designed to streamline processes and provide tailored information, spotlighting events and activities that cater to individuals eager to connect. Features often include calendars of happenings, dining and entertainment recommendations, and networking forums.

Tips for Overcoming Initial Loneliness

Experiencing loneliness during relocation or starting a new job is common, but effective strategies exist to mitigate these feelings. Maintaining connections with old friends can provide a comforting lifeline during transitions, offering emotional support that helps ease adjustment stress. Setting small, achievable social goals—such as attending one social event per week—can make meeting new people less intimidating.

Exploring new city spaces can also foster a sense of familiarity and connection. Whether it is finding a nearby café, visiting a local park, or browsing a farmers' market, these activities can help to combat feelings of solitude while encouraging the discovery of new favorite spots.

How to Attract New Friends

The importance of body language and overall attitude in attracting friends should not be underestimated. Maintaining an open posture, accompanied by eye contact and a warm smile, conveys approachability to others. Research in social psychology suggests that nonverbal communication plays a crucial role in forming first impressions (Burgoon, 2003).

Practical tips for initiating conversations could include offering genuine compliments or posing open-ended questions that encourage dialogue. Active listening is also vital; demonstrating sincere interest in others makes them feel valued and appreciated. Furthermore, creating inviting personal spaces—such as casual gatherings or dinner parties—can foster deeper connections and signal a willingness to form meaningful friendships.

Exercises to Develop a Positive Presence

Engaging in daily affirmations can be an effective way to build self-confidence and enhance overall demeanor and presence. Affirmations help reinforce a positive self-image, making social interactions less intimidating over time. Role-playing potential social interactions is another valuable exercise that can help individuals prepare for real-life engagements and alleviate anxiety in social settings.

While making friends in a new city or job can initially feel daunting, it offers profound opportunities for growth and connection. With the right mindset, proactive steps, and the willingness to embrace new experiences, anyone can cultivate a flourishing social circle. Each new friendship represents a new chapter—do not hesitate to turn the page!

By incorporating these strategies and insights from the academic literature, readers can navigate social integration challenges with optimism and purpose.

Networking Naturally

In today's interconnected world, the ability to network effectively is a vital skill that cuts across personal and professional contexts. Networking is not just about exchanging business cards or establishing LinkedIn connections; it embodies the art of building meaningful relationships.

When seen as a mutual benefit, networking shifts from being perceived as a daunting obligation toward a rewarding exchange of ideas, knowledge, and opportunities. In her work, Bourdieu's *Theory of Social*

Capital, sociologist Pierre Bourdieu (1986) argued that social networks carry their forms of capital; it is not just what you know but who you know that counts.

Strategies for Authentic Networking

To network authentically, individuals should start by identifying common interests that can serve as conversation starters. This can be as simple as discussing shared experiences or professional interests. For example, if you find yourself at a conference, use the events within it as conversation pieces. You can initiate deeper dialogues by sharing your takeaways from a workshop or discussing a speaker's insights.

Following up with new contacts is equally essential. Research by the American Society of Training and Development (ASTD) indicates that maintaining regular contact is crucial for establishing lasting connections (ASTD, 2010). A simple email thanking someone for their conversation or sharing an article relevant to their interests can convey genuine interest and a desire to maintain the relationship.

Participating in industry events, seminars, and workshops is also an invaluable strategy. These gatherings broaden your exposure to new ideas and offer rich opportunities to meet individuals who share similar professional aspirations and challenges. A *Harvard Business Review* study highlighted that face-to-face networking leads to stronger relationships than virtual interactions (HBR, 2015).

The Benefits of Creating a Network

The benefits of cultivating a robust professional network are manifold. A well-established network can unlock new career opportunities and provide access to resources that facilitate personal and professional growth. Increased visibility within a professional community can lead to career advancements, as referrals often arise from trusted connections.

A diverse network—encompassing different backgrounds, industries, and experiences—also offers a safety net of support and inspiration, enabling individuals to navigate career challenges more effectively. Research conducted by Granovetter (1973) demonstrated that weak ties often provide access to new information and opportunities that strong ties cannot offer.

Tips for Maintaining Professional Relationships

Building a professional relationship is just the beginning; nurturing these connections is equally, if not more important. Regularly checking in with your contacts helps foster a sense of continuity and support. This could involve sending periodic messages to inquire about their ventures or sharing valuable insights pertinent to their field.

Offering help, whether through sharing resources or extending introductions to other contacts, strengthens these bonds and positions you as a valuable asset within your network. Celebrating your contacts' achievements and milestones is a gentle reminder of shared journeys and successes. Whether it is a congratulatory message on a new job or an acknowledgment of a professional award, these gestures reinforce the relationship and cultivate goodwill.

By embracing the challenges and opportunities presented by new social environments, individuals can build meaningful connections that significantly enrich their lives personally and professionally. With a positive mindset and practical strategies, the journey toward friendship and community becomes an achievable adventure, paving the way for lasting bonds in all aspects of life. Effective networking is a journey, not a destination; it requires patience, authenticity, and an open heart.

With each connection you build, remember that you are not just expanding a network but enriching your life and the lives of others. Stay enthusiastic, keep growing, and watch the bonds you create flourish.

Conclusion

Stepping into a new city or a different career path provides a unique personal and professional growth opportunity. While a sense of intimidation may accompany the initial excitement, the journey of building a social network is filled with promise and potential.

Throughout this chapter, we have emphasized that the foundation of making meaningful connections begins with cultivating the right mindset. Viewing each new encounter and setting as a chance for growth equips you to face these changes enthusiastically rather than apprehensive. Transforming your outlook into welcoming and curious can pave the way for unexpected friendships and collaborations.

The practical strategies discussed—from engaging in community activities to leveraging digital platforms—serve as crucial tools for establishing a vibrant social base. You can meet like-minded individuals who share your passions by actively participating in local groups that align with your interests or joining professional meetups. Such shared experiences enrich your social life and deepen your fulfillment.

Moreover, we explored strategies to combat feelings of loneliness during periods of transition. Establishing small, manageable social goals—such as attending weekly local events or reconnecting with old friends—can ease the adjustment process and help maintain a sense of belonging. Remember, connecting with new and familiar faces can provide emotional support while navigating your new surroundings.

Networking, a vital skill in personal and professional realms, transcends beyond merely exchanging contacts. We have highlighted the art of authentic networking as an essential approach to building substantial relationships based on mutual interest and benefit. Recognizing that establishing and nurturing these connections often leads to new opportunities can significantly enhance your personal and career development.

As you embark on this journey, remember that building relationships is an ongoing process that requires patience, resilience, and commitment. Embrace the challenges that come your way, and actively seek the moments of connection. By increasing your social circle, you enrich your own life but also contribute to the lives of others—a cycle of positivity that fosters a strong community.

In essence, stepping into new arenas may present challenges, but with the right perspective and strategies, you can transform these into enriching experiences. Remember, each new friendship is a chapter waiting to be written. So, take a deep breath, step forward confidently, and let the connection adventure unfold. The friendships and opportunities you seek are out there, ready for you to discover. Keep your heart and mind open; you will be amazed at the connections coming your way.

References

American Society of Training and Development (ASTD). (2010). "The Networking Competency: Essential Skills for Personal and Professional Development."

Bourdieu, P. (1986). "The Forms of Capital." In J. Richardson (Ed.), *Handbook of Theory and Research for the Sociology of Education* (241–258). New York: Greenwood.

Burgoon, J. K. (2003). "Nonverbal Communication." In *The International Encyclopedia of Communication*.

Clary, E. G., Snyder, M., & Ridge, R. D. (1998). "Volunteers' Motivations: A Functional Approach." *Journal of Personality and Social Psychology*, 74 (6), 1516-1529.

Granovetter, M. (1973). The Strength of Weak Ties. American Journal of Sociology, 78(6), 1360-1380.

Harvard Business Review. (2015). "The Strength of Your Network: How to Get More Useful Advice."

Murray, S. L., & Manzo, L. C. (2015). "Shared Experiences and Personal Satisfaction: The Role of Activity Involvement in Social Bonds." *Journal of Social Issues*, 71 (4), 825-844.

Mastering Conversation

Mastering the art of conversation has never been more crucial. The foundation of enriching friendships lies in authentic and meaningful interactions. To cultivate deeper connections, individuals must first embrace the importance of authenticity.

Being genuine in conversations fosters trust and encourages others to reciprocate with openness, creating a safe space for vulnerability. Personal anecdotes can serve as powerful tools in this regard, inviting others to share their experiences and uncertainties. When someone admits their struggles or seeks advice, it opens the door for deeper dialogue, establishing a bond built on shared human experiences.

Storytelling may play a pivotal role in engaging conversations. Individuals can paint vivid pictures that captivate their listeners by sharing personal narratives. Each story should have a clear beginning, middle, and end, guiding the listener through an emotional journey.

Weaving in personal reflections enhances the storytelling experience and establishes an emotional connection.

Transitioning smoothly between topics is a skill that significantly contributes to deeper conversations. Individuals can guide discussions from light small talk toward deeper subjects by identifying natural segues based on shared interests. Open-ended statements present excellent opportunities for inviting more significant discussions, allowing the conversation to unfold organically.

Empathy in Conversations

Empathy is a vital bridge in fostering meaningful conversations, allowing individuals to connect on a deeper emotional level. It involves the ability to understand and empathize with another person's feelings, which can significantly enhance communication and connection.

Understanding Empathy

Empathy is a multifaceted skill that can be categorized into three essential components: Cognitive Empathy, Emotional Empathy, and Compassionate Empathy. Each component plays a crucial role in fostering deeper connections and creating a supportive environment, particularly in personal development and self-help contexts.

Cognitive Empathy is the intellectual understanding of another person's thoughts and perspectives. It involves recognizing what someone else thinks or feels without necessarily experiencing those emotions. For instance, when a friend recounts their struggles with anxiety, an empathetic response might include acknowledging their mental state by saying, "It sounds like you are overwhelmed right now." This statement illustrates Cognitive Empathy by demonstrating awareness of the friend's emotional landscape.

On the other hand, **Emotional Empathy** goes a step further by involving the emotional resonance with someone else's feelings. It is the ability to share and connect with another person's emotions, which can foster a sense of shared human experience. For example, if a colleague expresses sadness after a personal loss, an *Emotionally Empathetic* response could be, "I can see how heartbroken you must feel about your loss." This acknowledgment not only validates the other person's emotions but also reinforces the bond between both individuals.

Compassionate Empathy encapsulates the proactive element of understanding others' emotions and actions based on that insight. It is about being moved to help someone in need after experiencing their emotions. For instance, if one friend notices another struggling through a difficult time and responds with an offer to listen or provide support—such as saying, "I am here for you if you want to talk or need anything"—this reflects Compassionate Empathy. It emphasizes the importance of feeling empathy and translating that feeling into meaningful actions that can aid someone else.

Reflecting emotions and validating experiences are vital practices in effective communication that can enhance interpersonal connections. Paraphrasing what the other person has shared is a powerful method for demonstrating empathy during conversations. This technique affirms that one has been attentive and deepens the exchange.

For example, if a person expresses, "I feel like I am constantly battling stress at work," a thoughtful response could be, "So, you are saying that the pressure at your job is becoming difficult to manage." By restating their feelings accurately, one communicates that they have heard the person's words and comprehend the emotional weight behind those sentiments.

Thus, by actively cultivating these components of empathy—cognitive, Emotional, and Compassionate—individuals can develop stronger, more supportive relationships. This fosters an environment where open dialogue and mutual respect can thrive, significantly contributing to personal growth and emotional wellness.

Active Listening

Active listening forms the cornerstone of effective communication. It transcends the act of hearing and involves engaging with the speaker at a deeper level. Essential components of active listening include:

1. Maintaining Eye Contact: This non-verbal cue indicates that you are focused and present in the conversation.

2. Nodding: Simple nods can show understanding and encourage the speaker to continue.

3. Allowing Pauses: Giving the speaker time to collect their thoughts without interrupting demonstrates respect and attentiveness.

To sharpen your active listening skills, practice summarizing key points before responding. For instance, after your colleague explains a difficult project, summarizing their main concerns before offering your thoughts shows that you are engaged and invested in the discussion. Additionally, asking clarifying questions—such as, "Can you explain what you mean by that?"—ensures you fully comprehend the speaker's message.

Mindful listening in everyday interactions—such as during meetings, casual conversations, or family discussions—can help hone these skills, paving the way for genuine connections. The benefits of active listening extend beyond mere comprehension; it fosters a sense of being heard and valued, essential ingredients in building trust. Effective listening allows relationships to flourish on a solid foundation of understanding by reducing misunderstandings and conflict.

Encouraging Others to Open Up

Questions are a vital tool for inviting deeper insights during conversations. The ability to ask the right questions can lead to more enriching discussions and foster greater openness. Open-ended questions, in particular, encourage the other person to explore topics freely, igniting a sense of curiosity that can enhance the dialogue.

Formulating effective questions requires thoughtfulness. Avoiding leading or loaded questions is critical for maintaining neutrality and encouraging honest responses. For instance, instead of asking, "Don't you think that project will fail?" you could ask, "What are your thoughts on the potential challenges of that project?" This approach fosters an open environment for discussion.

Tailoring questions to fit the context and flow of

the conversation can further improve engagement. Using follow-up questions, such as "Can you tell me more about that?" or "What led you to that conclusion?" deepens the conversation and shows genuine interest in the speaker's thoughts. Building on previous answers, you can guide the dialogue into unexplored territories, demonstrating attentiveness and commitment to the exchange.

Empathy, active listening, and thoughtful questioning are crucial to effective conversation. By leveraging these skills, individuals can foster deeper connections, enhance understanding, and create an environment where meaningful dialogue thrives. Embracing these practices can lead to enriched relationships, both personally and professionally.

By integrating the principles of empathy and active listening, you can transform your conversations, paving the way for stronger, more meaningful relationships. Apply these concepts to your daily interactions, and watch your connections flourish!

Questions for Various Scenarios

To empower readers in navigating conversations, consider these versatile questions tailored for different scenarios:

To initiate conversations at social gatherings: "What is a recent passion project you have been working on?"

To deepen professional interactions, ask: "What led you to pursue this career path?"

For exploring personal interests or passions: "What experience has shaped your perspective on this topic?"

Individuals can transform their interactions by mastering the art of conversation through these outlined techniques and principles. The world is a vast tapestry of potential friendships waiting to unfold, and each conversation is a thread that weaves this tapestry together. With a sense of intention, empathy, and curiosity, anyone can foster deeper connections that enrich their lives and those of others.

References

Brown, B. (2012). ***Daring Greatly: How the Courage to Be Vulnerable Transforms the Way We Live, Love, Parent, and Lead***. Gotham Books.

Goleman, D. (1995). ***Emotional Intelligence: Why It Can Matter More Than IQ***. Bantam.

Rogers, C. R. (1980). ***A Way of Being***. Houghton Mifflin Harcourt.

Stein, J. (2013). ***The Power of Empathy: A Practical Guide to Creating a More Compassionate***

World. The Empathy Institute.

Embracing Cultural Diversity

In a world increasingly marked by cultural diversity, the ability to build and nurture friendships across cultural boundaries has become more important than ever. Central to this endeavor is the practice of empathy.

Empathy enables individuals to connect on a fundamental human level, transcending the often visible barriers erected by varied backgrounds. It involves an effort to understand and share the feelings of others, making it a powerful tool in cross-cultural interactions.

Practicing perspective-taking is a vital component of empathy. Individuals can foster connections that may otherwise remain distant by genuinely trying to understand differing cultural viewpoints. This process goes beyond mere acknowledgment of different customs; it requires an active listening approach, inviting individuals to immerse themselves in the cultural narratives and experiences of others. Friendships can flourish through compelling storytelling and personal accounts, creating bridges where walls once stood.

Open-mindedness complements empathy as a crucial ingredient for cultivating cultural understanding. An open mind can lead to richer, more meaningful interactions and friendships. By challenging personal assumptions and stereotypes, individuals can create inclusive environments where everyone feels valued. Embracing cultural differences becomes an opportunity for learning, urging friends to share new experiences and traditions.

To nurture empathy and open-mindedness, individuals can engage in practical exercises that broaden their horizons. Participating in cultural exchange programs or learning a new language exposes individuals to diverse perspectives, fostering connections through shared experiences. Additionally, attending cultural workshops or seminars can enhance understanding of various customs, providing a conducive platform for dialogue and interaction.

Inspiring anecdotes illustrate how successful cultural bridging can occur. Numerous individuals have formed deep, lasting friendships through cultural immersion. These stories often highlight the power of empathy in overcoming misunderstandings and establishing connections that enrich lives. Each narrative serves as a reminder that friendship is possible regardless of cultural disparities.

Navigating Cultural Norms

Understanding cultural norms is essential for preventing misunderstandings and fostering respect in our increasingly interconnected world. Cultural norms are the unwritten rules that guide behavior in social contexts, yet they can vary greatly from one culture to another. This section will examine the significance of these norms, focusing on nonverbal communication, time management, social etiquette, and strategies to promote cultural sensitivity.

Nonverbal Communication

Nonverbal communication encompasses many signals, including gestures, facial expressions, eye contact, and body language. These nonverbal cues are crucial in conveying messages and emotions without using spoken words. However, interpreting these signals can significantly differ across various cultures, highlighting the importance of cultural awareness in communication.

For instance, in many Western cultures, maintaining direct eye contact is often associated with confidence and sincerity. Individuals are taught that maintaining eye contact demonstrates engagement and honesty. In contrast, in certain Asian or Indigenous cultures, direct eye contact can be interpreted as disrespectful or confrontational. In these contexts, individuals might avoid prolonged eye contact to exhibit politeness and humility.

To navigate these cultural nuances effectively, one must observe the social dynamics in one's surroundings. An example can be seen in interactions with individuals from Native American cultures, where one may notice a tendency to avoid direct eye contact.

This behavior is generally rooted in cultural practices that emphasize respect and attentiveness. For Native Americans, engaging in a conversation without constant eye contact can reflect a deeper respect for the speaker and the shared space.

Acknowledging and adapting to these nonverbal cues is a sign of respect and can foster a deeper connection between individuals from different backgrounds. Mindful of the nonverbal communication styles prevalent in various cultures can enhance interpersonal skills.

This awareness paves the way for more meaningful conversations, ultimately enriching relationships and a broader understanding of diverse perspectives. Being attuned to nonverbal communication is vital to personal development and effective communication in an increasingly interconnected world.

The Importance of Punctuality

A critical aspect of cultural norms is the perception of time, which plays a significant role in shaping interpersonal interactions and professional relationships across different societies. In many cultures, punctuality is a crucial indicator of professionalism and respect for others.

For example, in countries such as Germany and Switzerland, being on time is a value deeply ingrained in their societal fabric. Individuals in these cultures often perceive lateness as disrespectful and indicative of a lack of commitment or seriousness. In a business meeting in Germany, arriving even a few minutes late can disrupt the flow of conversation and create an unfavorable impression.

Conversely, time can be viewed more flexibly in many Latin American and Middle Eastern cultures. In these regions, a more relaxed attitude toward punctuality allows social interactions to unfold organically without the strict constraints of a clock. For instance, in Brazil, gatherings often commence with a degree of fluidity; it is common for attendees to arrive after the stated start time. Understanding and adapting to this flexibility can help individuals establish stronger connections and foster better collaboration in these contexts.

Consider preparing for a meeting with a colleague from Japan, where punctuality is paramount. Arriving punctually can show respect and set a positive tone for the entire interaction. Conversely, acknowledging the local approach to time in a Brazilian business environment can facilitate more fluid and enjoyable exchanges.

By recognizing these cultural differences regarding time, individuals can navigate relationships more effectively, demonstrate cultural sensitivity, and enhance their personal and professional interactions. This knowledge can be a powerful tool for personal growth, enabling individuals to expand their cultural awareness and thrive in diverse social environments.

Social Etiquette

Social etiquette encompasses a range of behaviors, including greetings, dining practices, and gift-giving traditions. Each culture has its own rules that define how people should interact socially. Familiarity with these customs can enhance relationships and prevent unintentional faux pas.

Example: In many Asian societies, gift-giving is integral to relationship-building. Giving a gift is not merely transactional; it is steeped in tradition and meaning. When presenting a gift, offer it with both hands as a sign of respect. In Middle Eastern cultures, understanding dining etiquette, such as refraining from eating with your left hand—a practice considered impolite—can also facilitate smoother social interactions.

Fostering Cultural Sensitivity

Cultural sensitivity is crucial in fostering social connections and friendships. It involves a commitment to understanding and respecting diverse cultures' unique traditions and values. To cultivate cultural sensitivity, consider the following strategies:

1. Learn and Observe: Learn about the cultures around you. Observe how people interact, including their nonverbal cues and approach to time.

2. Ask Questions: When unsure about cultural expectations, do not hesitate to ask questions. Most people appreciate genuine curiosity and willingness to learn.

3. Avoid Stereotyping: Recognize the individuality of cultures. While cultural norms might provide a general guideline, personal preferences can vary significantly.

By being mindful of cultural norms and adapting your behavior, you create opportunities for deeper connections and mutual respect. Understanding and adapting to cultural norms will help you avoid misunderstandings and enrich your personal and professional relationships, ultimately facilitating more harmonious interactions in a diverse world.

Building Multicultural Friendships

Building multicultural friendships is a transformative process that extends well beyond personal enjoyment. These relationships are crucial in broadening our perspectives and enriching our lives. Engaging with individuals from diverse backgrounds exposes us to varying worldviews and philosophies, ultimately fostering profound personal growth and facilitating self-reflection.

The Benefits of Multicultural Friendships

Multicultural friendships present a wealth of benefits that can significantly enhance personal growth and development. Research has shown that engaging with individuals from various cultural backgrounds fosters creativity. According to Nussbaum (2017), these interactions challenge people to step outside their comfort zones, essential for innovative thinking. When confronted with different perspectives and experiences, individuals are encouraged to think more broadly, leading to the exploration of new ideas and solutions.

For instance, a brainstorming session with diverse voices typically yields more concepts than a homogeneous group might. This dynamic is evident in the creative industries, where teams comprising individuals from diverse cultural backgrounds frequently produce groundbreaking work.

Moreover, multicultural relationships play a crucial role in developing emotional intelligence, empathy, and adaptability—qualities that are increasingly necessary in today's interconnected world. Emotional intelligence allows individuals to recognize and manage their own emotions while understanding and empathizing with the feelings of others. Building friendships with people from diverse cultures enhances one's ability to navigate complex emotional landscapes, necessitating a deeper understanding of varying cultural nuances and communication styles.

A study published in the *Journal of Social Issues* further underscores the importance of multicultural friendships by revealing that individuals who cultivate such relationships report higher levels of well-being and life satisfaction (Duggan et al., 2019). This suggests that bridging cultural divides enriches one's social life and contributes to overall mental well-being.

For example, someone who forms a friendship with someone from a different background may find joy in shared experiences, even as they learn and grow from the differences. Such friendships foster personal resilience and adaptability, enabling individuals to confidently navigate a rapidly changing world.

Thus, embracing multicultural friendships can lead to a myriad of positive outcomes—enhancing creativity, nurturing emotional intelligence, and promoting a higher quality of life. Individuals can enrich their lives by seeking out and celebrating diverse relationships while contributing to a more inclusive and understanding society. The journey toward building these connections broadens horizons and fosters a sense of belonging that transcends cultural boundaries.

Initiating/Sustaining Multicultural Friendships

To effectively initiate and sustain multicultural friendships, it is essential to apply some practical tips:

1. Finding Common Ground: Start by identifying shared interests. Participation in hobbies, academic pursuits, or community activities can create a strong foundation for meaningful connections. For example, joining a local cooking class or participating in cultural festivals can facilitate activities that bring people together over shared passions.

2. Communicating with Patience and Understanding: Open and effective communication is essential in overcoming potential language barriers and cultural misunderstandings. When encountering different communication styles or language nuances, patience can go a long way. Tools like Google Translate or language exchange apps can help alleviate some of the barriers when people express a willingness to learn and understand one another.

3. Navigating Challenges with Grace: Friendships may encounter challenges, such as misinterpretations arising from cultural misunderstandings. Approaching these situations with empathy and an open heart strengthens ties and creates opportunities for dialogue, allowing individuals to emerge with greater understanding and resilience.

4. Balancing Identity and Adaptation: As you forge multicultural friendships, it is vital to balance your cultural identity while embracing the richness of others. This journey may be complex, but it leads to friendships that are not only rewarding but also offer deeper insights into both your culture and those of your friends.

Stories of

Multicultural Friendships

Numerous case studies underscore the success of multicultural friendships. One illustrative example features two individuals hailing from different continents: one from Africa and the other from South America. These two friends met during an international volunteer program, where the shared goal of community service provided a common ground that transcended their differences.

As their friendship developed, both individuals began to exchange their life stories, revealing the rich tapestry of their respective cultures. Through deep conversations, they navigated their challenges together, spoke candidly about their backgrounds, and celebrated the unique traditions that defined their identities.

This exchange not only strengthened their bond but also enriched their perspectives. When they faced personal struggles in their own lives, they leaned on each other for support, offering understanding and encouragement that transcended geographical boundaries.

Upon returning to their home countries, these friends maintained their relationship, continuing to share their experiences and insights through regular communication. Their stories serve as a powerful reminder of the profound impact that mutual learning and respect can have on personal growth. In a world that can often feel divided, their connection exemplifies how navigating differences and cherishing shared experiences can foster lasting friendships.

Embracing cultural diversity through empathy and open-mindedness has become vital in today's interconnected society. Multicultural friendships not only enhance individual personal and emotional development but also contribute to a broader understanding of humanity's diverse tapestry. As individuals embark on the journey of building these friendships, it is essential to recognize that friendship transcends borders.

The process of navigating cultural differences may present challenges, but it also yields rewarding experiences. By welcoming new perspectives and forming genuine connections, individuals can embark on a fulfilling journey that ultimately enriches their lives and those of those around them.

References

Adler, P. S., & Gundersen, A. (2007). *International Dimensions of Organizational Behavior.* Mason, OH: Thomson/South-Western.

Duggan, M., Ellison, N. B., Lampe, C., Lenhart, A., & Madden, M. (2019). "Social Media and the Cost of Caring: A Study on Multicultural Interactions." *Journal of Social Issues*, 75(3), 562–586.

Hall, E. T. (1976). *Beyond Culture*. New York: Anchor Books.

- Hofstede, G., & Hofstede, G. J. (2005). *Cultures and Organizations: Software of the Mind.* New York: McGraw-Hill.

Nussbaum, M. (2017). Creative Abundance: The Importance of Multicultural Friendships in Creativity. New York, NY: HarperCollins.

Managing Social Anxiety

Forming connections can sometimes feel daunting, particularly for those grappling with social anxiety. Within this chapter, mindfulness emerges as a powerful ally, helping individuals navigate social settings with greater ease and confidence.

Staying Present in Social Settings

In the field of personal development, individuals often confront the challenges posed by social anxiety, particularly during social interactions. However, mastering the art of staying present can greatly alleviate these feelings. Mindfulness practices emerge as invaluable tools in this endeavor, providing individuals the means to anchor themselves in the present moment.

Focusing on the present moment rather than

becoming consumed by spiraling anxious thoughts can help individuals cultivate a greater sense of calm and clarity. This approach helps reduce overwhelming emotions and enhances their ability to engage more fully and authentically with others. As they embrace mindfulness, they discover newfound opportunities for connection, transforming potentially stressful social situations into enriching experiences.

Through consistent mindfulness practice, individuals can gradually overcome the burdens of social anxiety, leading to a more fulfilling social life. With each mindful moment, they take steps toward greater self-awareness, improving their interactions and overall emotional well-being.

Understanding Mindfulness

Mindfulness is the non-judgmental awareness of one's thoughts, feelings, and sensory experiences unfolding in the present moment. Practicing mindfulness involves focusing on immediate sensory experiences, such as the sounds surrounding you or the texture of an object you touch.

For example, during a social gathering, you might consciously listen to the laughter in the background or feel the warmth of a cup in your hands. Grounding yourself in these sensations can create a buffer against anxiety, allowing you to regain composure and foster more meaningful interactions.

Observing Without Judgment

An essential component of mindfulness is cultivating a non-judgmental awareness of one's thoughts. This practice encourages individuals to observe their emotions and mental processes without attaching labels of "good" or "bad" to them. For instance, when feelings of anxiety arise, a person can imagine these emotions as clouds drifting through the sky. By adopting this perspective, they can create a metaphorical distance between themselves and their anxiety, allowing them to acknowledge its presence without becoming overwhelmed.

This method is particularly valuable because it helps to reduce the intensity of these feelings. Instead of grappling with anxiety as a threatening entity, the individual learns to view it as a transient experience. Just like clouds, emotions can roll in and out, which fosters a sense of acceptance and resilience. This shift in perception can lead to a profound transformation in one's relationship with anxiety, enabling a person to approach their feelings with curiosity rather than fear.

Research in psychology underscores the importance of this nonjudgmental awareness. According to a study by Keng, Smoski, and Robins

(2011), simply acknowledging emotions—regardless of their nature—can empower individuals to manage anxiety more effectively. This approach facilitates emotional regulation and cultivates a greater sense of overall well-being. By practicing mindfulness in this way, individuals often find themselves better equipped to navigate life's ups and downs, leading to increased emotional resilience and a more balanced state of mind.

Observing thoughts and feelings can significantly enhance personal growth, providing individuals with tools to transform their mental landscape. This practice encourages people to accept their emotions as a natural part of life rather than obstacles to overcome, enabling them to live more fully in the present moment.

Breathing Techniques for Calm

Breathing techniques serve as practical tools for immediate anxiety relief. One such method is the 4-7-8 breathing technique. Here is how to practice it:

1. Inhale through the nose for four seconds.

2. Hold your breath for seven seconds.

3. Exhale slowly through the mouth for eight seconds.

This controlled breathing not only alleviates immediate anxiety but can also help establish a more relaxed state of mind for ongoing social interactions.

Another useful technique is box breathing. The steps are:

1. Inhale for four seconds.
2. Hold your breath for four seconds.
3. Exhale for four seconds.
4. Hold again for four seconds.

This structured approach encourages relaxation and serves as a handy skill to use when anxiety starts to escalate.

Improving Engagement Through Mindfulness

Mindfulness is a powerful tool for enhancing one's presence in social settings, significantly fostering deeper engagement and attentiveness during conversations. When individuals practice active listening, free from mental distractions, they tend to connect more meaningfully with others. This involves fully concentrating on the rhythm of the speaker's voice, the nuances of their speech, and the emotions conveyed through their words. By resisting the temptation to allow random thoughts to intrude, individuals can transform social interactions from routine exchanges into enriching experiences.

A practical example of this can be seen in a

simple conversation where one individual shares a personal story. Instead of mentally crafting a response while the other speaks, a mindful listener focuses intently on what is being said.

They may notice the speaker's body language, the passion in their voice, and the underlying emotions in their narrative. This level of engagement validates the speaker's feelings and inspires a deeper, more authentic dialogue.

Furthermore, grounding techniques can be critical in maintaining a sense of presence during social interactions. Techniques such as tuning into one's breathtaking, slow, deliberate inhales and exhales can help anchor individuals in the moment. Additionally, becoming mindful of physical sensations, such as the sensation of the ground beneath one's feet or the texture of the chair one is sitting on, can create a sense of stability and calm.

When individuals utilize these grounding strategies, they become fully engaged with those around them. In this heightened state of awareness, conversations can flourish, leading to richer connections and more fulfilling social experiences. By embracing mindfulness in social settings, individuals not only enhance their interactions but also cultivate a more profound appreciation for the shared moments that shape their lives.

Integrating Mindfulness into Daily Life

Mindfulness can be incorporated into your daily routine through practical and enjoyable activities, such as mindful walking or mindful eating. In these activities, you pay close attention to the sensations involved, fostering a more mindful approach to everyday life. For instance, while eating, take the time to savor each bite, noticing the flavors and textures, which fosters a sense of gratitude.

Additionally, daily gratitude journaling is a powerful practice that encourages focused awareness. By reflecting on positive experiences and jotting them down, individuals can cultivate a habit of mindfulness that extends throughout their day. This practice can enhance your overall perspective, helping to keep anxiety at bay and replacing it with a sense of appreciation and contentment.

Cultivating mindfulness and utilizing specific techniques can transform the experience of social interactions for those struggling with anxiety. You can cultivate a calmer and more confident social presence by anchoring yourself in the present moment, utilizing breathing techniques, engaging in focused listening, and incorporating mindful practices into your daily routine. As you embark on this journey of self-discovery and personal growth, remember that each moment presents an opportunity for connection and development.

Building Self-Compassion

One of the most significant barriers to forming genuine friendships often stems from the pervasive fear of judgment. This fear is deeply rooted in self-criticism and the societal pressures we face, which can exert undue influence over our self-esteem and perceptions of adequacy.

It is crucial to recognize and understand the origins of this fear, as it frequently arises from cultural norms that glorify perfection and implicitly promote negative self-talk. In this light, cultivating self-compassion becomes an essential strategy for overcoming these challenges.

Understanding the Fear of Judgment

The fear of judgment is a multifaceted emotion influenced by various factors, including personal experiences, societal expectations, and deeply ingrained beliefs. Individuals are often shaped by the environments in which they grow up. For instance, a child raised in an atmosphere where explicit or subtle criticism is prevalent may develop a lingering sense of self-doubt. This ongoing exposure to negative feedback can cultivate an internal narrative that convinces them they are never adequate, resulting in a debilitating fear of not meeting the often unrealistic standards set by others.

Moreover, societal norms significantly contribute to this fear. Various cultures promote specific ideals regarding success and behavior, creating a pressure cooker of expectations that individuals feel compelled to navigate. For example, one might believe they must follow certain career paths, maintain specific relationship statuses, or conform to certain physical appearances to be considered successful or valuable. Such societal pressures can intensify feelings of inadequacy and fear, causing individuals to hesitate to present their authentic selves or pursue their true passions.

Additionally, internalized beliefs—those ideas that individuals unconsciously accept about themselves and their capabilities—add another layer of complexity to this emotional landscape. Someone who has been judged repeatedly, whether by parents, peers, or society, may internalize the notion of being unworthy or flawed. This perception can manifest as a fear of criticism, holding them back from taking necessary risks or seizing opportunities that could lead to personal growth.

Recognizing these underlying factors is crucial for overcoming the fear of judgment. By understanding how past experiences and societal influences have shaped their self-perception, individuals can empower themselves to challenge and reshape these internal narratives. Cultivating self-awareness and fostering a compassionate mindset can enable them to gradually embrace vulnerability and approach life with courage, liberated from the constraints of judgment.

The Role of Self-Compassion

Self-compassion is a powerful antidote to the pervasive fear of judgment that many individuals experience. Rooted in the work of psychologist Kristin Neff, self-compassion entails treating oneself with the same kindness, understanding, and support one would naturally extend to a close friend. By consciously practicing self-compassion, individuals can effectively counter negative thoughts that often fuel self-criticism while building resilience in the face of life's challenges.

This framework recognizes personal struggles as a shared aspect of the human experience. When individuals acknowledge that everyone faces difficulties, it becomes easier to diminish feelings of isolation and foster a sense of connection. Self-compassion encourages individuals to understand that they are not alone in their struggles but are part of a larger community navigating through similar challenges.

For example, individuals may find themselves besieged by self-critical thoughts when confronted with failure—such as underperforming in a professional setting or experiencing an embarrassing moment in social interactions. These thoughts can often lead to shame, embarrassment, or inadequacy. However, adopting a self-compassionate mindset can transform these experiences into valuable opportunities for growth and learning.

Instead of succumbing to damaging thoughts that label them as a "failure," individuals practicing self-compassion might reframe their internal dialogue. They could remind themselves, "I am doing my best, and it is perfectly okay to make mistakes." This shift in perspective not only alleviates the burden of self-judgment but also enables a more open acknowledgment of one's humanity and imperfections, thereby paving the way for greater emotional resilience and personal growth

Actionable Strategies to Cultivate Self-Compassion

Developing self-compassion is a skill that can be cultivated through various actionable strategies:

1. Self-Compassionate Meditations: Guided meditations focused on self-kindness and acceptance can help reshape negative thought patterns. Research by

Neff and Germer (2013) highlighted that participants who engaged in self-compassion meditations reported lower levels of anxiety and increased emotional resilience.

2. Affirmations: Positive affirmations that reinforce self-worth and acknowledge imperfections can be powerful tools. For instance, repeating phrases like, "I am enough just as I am," in moments of self-doubt can build a more compassionate internal dialogue.

3. Mindful Awareness: Practicing mindfulness allows individuals to observe their thoughts without judgment. By acknowledging negative self-talk, one can begin to distance their identity from these thoughts, recognizing that they do not define their worth.

4. Embracing Common Humanity: Reminding oneself that struggles are universal can create a sense of connectedness. Understanding that others face similar challenges can alleviate feelings of isolation and promote empathy.

5. Journaling: Writing about experiences and emotions can create clarity around negative self-perceptions. A gratitude journal, which focuses on positive aspects and achievements, can shift one's perspective over time.

By implementing these practices, individuals often find that self-compassion naturally leads to decreased anxiety and heightened social confidence. Creating an internal environment free from harsh self-judgment enables more authentic connections with others, allowing friendships to flourish without the heavy burden of fear and self-doubt.

Building self-compassion is not just about fostering a kinder relationship with oneself; it is also about opening doors to meaningful connections with others. Recognizing and addressing the fear of judgment allows you to cultivate a sense of belonging and authenticity in their social interactions.

Real-life Practice and Solutions

Navigating social anxiety scenarios involves employing practical, actionable solutions tailored to common triggers that many individuals face. Situations like initiating conversations at social gatherings or voicing opinions in group settings can provoke significant anxiety. By understanding these triggers and implementing specific strategies, individuals can approach these challenges with increased confidence and composure.

Preparation: A Key Strategy

Preparation is a fundamental strategy in alleviating anxiety related to social interactions. One effective method is to develop conversation starters in advance. For instance, consider preparing a few open-ended questions or comments about current events, shared interests, or even light-hearted anecdotes.

This foresight can prevent one from feeling unprepared or overwhelmed when interacting with others. For example, if you know you will be attending a networking event, you could prepare questions like, "What is the most interesting project you are working on right now?" or "Have you read any good books lately?"

Additionally, role-playing scenarios with a trusted friend or family member can be incredibly beneficial. This practice enables individuals to simulate social situations they anticipate facing, thereby helping them become more acclimated to the interaction dynamics. Rehearsing potential conversations helps you to reduce the anxiety associated with spontaneity and develop a greater sense of agency.

Gradual Exposure

Another powerful technique for managing social anxiety is gradual exposure to challenging social situations. This approach involves deliberately and systematically placing oneself in mildly anxiety-inducing situations, progressively increasing the difficulty level as comfort grows.

One might start by attending a small gathering

before advancing to larger events. This incremental exposure helps to desensitize the individual to anxiety triggers, gradually building confidence and resilience.

Reflecting on past experiences is also crucial in the growth process. After navigating a social interaction, take a moment to self-assess what went well and what could be improved. Journaling about these encounters can foster growth, allowing individuals to recognize patterns and learn from each engagement.

Inspirational Success Stories

Success stories from individuals who have effectively managed their social anxiety can serve as inspiring examples for others facing similar challenges. One notable example is a person who struggled to speak up during group discussions. This individual began with small, manageable steps, such as sharing thoughts in low-pressure settings, like small gatherings with friends. As they practiced, their confidence grew. Over time, they became more comfortable expressing themselves and eventually found themselves leading discussions in larger groups.

These personal experiences illustrate the transformative power of overcoming social fears. By employing strategies such as mindfulness and self-compassion, individuals can create deeper, more meaningful friendships and widen their social networks. Such narratives not only encourage those who are struggling but also provide a clear demonstration that significant change is achievable through consistent effort and the right mindset.

Conclusion

As we conclude this chapter on managing social anxiety, it is essential to remember that the journey toward increased social confidence is both personal and unique. Social anxiety can feel isolating, but with the right tools and strategies, you can cultivate a sense of ease in connecting with others. By integrating mindfulness practices into your daily routines, you can ground yourself in the present moment, deflecting anxious thoughts and feelings that often cloud social interactions.

Embracing self-compassion is equally vital; understanding that everyone faces challenges in social settings normalizes your experience. This chapter has introduced several techniques, from mindful breathing exercises to positive affirmations, which can help you navigate social situations with resilience and poise. By reminding yourself that imperfection is part of the human experience, you will find it easier to approach new interactions with an open heart rather than a fearful mind.

Moreover, preparation and gradual exposure are actionable strategies that can empower you to confront your fears in a structured way. By practicing conversation starters and gradually entering more complex social scenarios, you cultivate confidence with every interaction. The inspirational success stories shared in this chapter serve as a testament to the transformative power of these practices, demonstrating that overcoming social anxiety is not only possible but also achievable.

As you move forward, remember to be gentle with yourself. Growth takes time, and each small step you take is a victory worth celebrating. By applying the tools discussed in this chapter, you will discover that social settings can become opportunities for genuine connection and enrichment. Every moment spent interacting with others is an opportunity for personal growth, fostering not only your social skills but also your overall well-being.

Allow this chapter to serve as a stepping stone in your self-help journey—embracing the skills and insights gained here can lead to profound changes in how you interact with others. Your path to managing social anxiety is not just about facing fears; it is about unlocking the potential for authentic relationships and a fulfilling social life. Keep these practices close at hand, and remember that you are capable of navigating the social landscape with grace and confidence.

References

Brown, B. (2012). Daring Greatly: How the Courage to Be Vulnerable Transforms the Way We Live, Love, Parent, and Lead. Gotham Books.

Germer, C. K., & Neff, K. D. (2013). "Self-Compassion in Clinical Practice." *Journal of Clinical Psychology*, 69(8), 856-867.

Keng, S. L., Smoski, M. J., & Robins, C. J. (2011). "Effects of Mindfulness on Psychological Health: A Review of Empirical Studies." *Clinical Psychology Review*, 31(6), 1041-1056.

Morrissette, P. J. (2005). Coping With Social Anxiety: A Comprehensive Guide for Overcoming the Challenges of Social Anxiety Disorder. New York: New Harbinger Publications.

McKay, M., Davis, M., & Fanning, P. (2011). *Messages: The Communication Skills Book*. New York: New Harbinger Publications.

Neff, K. D. (2011). Self-Compassion: The Proven Power of Being Kind to Yourself. New York: William Morrow Paperbacks.

Neff, K. D., & Germer, C. K. (2013). "A Pilot Study and Randomized Controlled Trial of the Mindful Self-Compassion Program." *Journal of Clinical Psychology*, 69(1), 28-44.

Rachman, S. (2013). *Fear and Courage*. New York: W. W. Norton & Company.

Existing Friendships

In a world that often feels fast-paced and disconnected, the significance of maintaining regular communication in friendships cannot be overstated. Consistent contact strengthens bonds and prevents friendships from drifting apart.

Establishing habits such as scheduling recurring monthly or bi-weekly meetups can create opportunities for meaningful interactions. Furthermore, leveraging technology, such as video calls, can bridge the physical distance gap, ensuring that friends can maintain their connection no matter where they are.

Meaningful catch-ups extend beyond the mere exchange of daily pleasantries. Engaging in joint activities or hobbies can invite deeper conversations and mutual enjoyment. Suggestions for reconnecting may include planning hikes, cooking together, or attending local events and workshops that interest both friends.

By participating in these activities, individuals share experiences and create lasting memories that enhance their friendship. When planning catch-up sessions, consider the following:

1. Nature Walks or Hikes: Choose a scenic location and walk or hike together. The natural environment sets a relaxed tone, and physical activity can inspire open discussion about life experiences and changes.

2. Cooking Together: Invite a friend to cook a meal. This interactive approach encourages teamwork and communication. Choose a recipe with sentimental value or try something new to add an element of adventure.

3. Attending Workshops or Classes: Identify mutual interests, such as art, cooking, or personal development, and sign up for a local workshop or class. Shared learning experiences can stimulate conversation and help both friends discover new facets of each other.

4. Game Nights: Organize a game night featuring board games or card games. The playful atmosphere fosters laughter and camaraderie, creating a comfortable environment for sharing personal updates about one's life.

5. Coffee Catch-Up: Sometimes simplicity is best. Arrange a casual coffee meetup where you can talk openly over a shared beverage. This straightforward approach can

You can successfully reconnect with old friends by engaging in meaningful activities and practicing open communication techniques. Remember that time and effort are investments in invaluable relationships. Each step you take towards rekindling these connections can lead to enriching experiences and lasting memories.

The Role of Active Listening

Active listening plays a critical role in nurturing close friendships. It involves being fully present and engaged during interactions. Most people can delve deeper into their friends' thoughts and feelings by using open-ended questions, thus facilitating a richer dialogue. Reflecting on what has been heard demonstrates understanding and validation, reinforcing the bond. Through these practices, friends can significantly improve the quality of their conversations.

Effective communication is essential in any friendship. Active listening, which involves being fully present during conversations, can significantly enhance reconnecting. Use these techniques:

Open-Ended Questions: Invite your friend to share more about their life by asking open-ended questions. Instead of asking, "Did you have a good weekend?" try, "What have you been up to lately that excites you?"

Paraphrasing: Reflect on what your friend shares to demonstrate your understanding. For instance, say, "It sounds like you faced some challenges at work. How did you handle that?"

Validating Feelings: Acknowledge your friend's feelings and experiences. A simple "That sounds tough" can make a significant difference, reinforcing the connection and showing that you care.

Tips for Balancing Time with Friends

Effective time management is crucial for individuals seeking to maintain and nurture connections with multiple friends. Research in the field of social psychology indicates that friendships play a vital role in emotional well-being and overall happiness (Dunbar, 2010). Individuals who prioritize friendships can create stronger, more meaningful relationships, thus enhancing their social support networks.

Prioritizing Connections: To manage friendships effectively, individuals should reflect on which relationships require more attention. This could involve evaluating past interactions and identifying friends who may feel neglected or with whom one wishes to reconnect.

According to a study by Holt-Lunstad et al.

(2010), strong social relationships significantly contribute to decreased mortality risk and improved physical health. Therefore, individuals should focus on nurturing those friendships that bring them joy, support, and fulfillment.

For example, suppose someone realizes they have not spoken to an old college friend in several years. In that case, they might prioritize that connection by contacting first, arranging a coffee catch-up, or initiating a virtual chat. This deliberate approach helps recalibrate personal social priorities and fosters satisfaction and belonging.

Group Gatherings: Incorporating group gatherings into one's social calendar is another effective way to maximize social time. Group gatherings not only allow individuals to connect with multiple friends simultaneously, but they can also enhance feelings of community and shared experiences. Organizing events such as potluck dinners, game nights, or outdoor picnics can allow friends to rekindle their bonds in a relaxed and enjoyable atmosphere.

Research by Wesselmann et al. (2012) highlights that social gatherings can increase social cohesion, reinforcing the strength of relationships when people engage in collective activities. By creating an environment where friends can socialize together, participants can enjoy camaraderie and belonging.

For instance, a person might find that hosting a

monthly dinner party to which various friends are invited preserves existing friendships and fosters new connections among attendees. This dynamic approach enhances social interactions and builds a stronger sense of community, which is particularly beneficial in today's fast-paced world.

Individuals can effectively manage their time and social lives by prioritizing meaningful friendships and fostering them through group gatherings. This deliberate approach strengthens bonds and enhances one's overall quality of life.

By understanding these principles, individuals can cultivate richer, more fulfilling friendships that positively contribute to their lives.

Handling Conflicts with Grace

It is essential to recognize that conflicts are an inevitable aspect of any close relationship. They represent opportunities for growth and understanding if navigated thoughtfully. By understanding common triggers and patterns in disputes, individuals can approach conflicts with a mindset geared toward resolution rather than confrontation. Here are some simple suggestions to help you deal with conflicts more gracefully:

Recognize Triggers: Take a moment to understand what typically triggers arguments between you and others. Knowing these triggers can help you be better prepared when conflicts arise.

Shift Your Mindset: Instead of approaching conflicts with a confrontational attitude, adopt a mindset focused on finding a solution. This change in perspective can make a big difference.

Use 'I' Statements: When expressing your feelings during a disagreement, use statements that start with "I" rather than "you." For example, say, "I feel hurt when..." instead of "You always..." This simple shift helps convey your emotions without placing blame, making the conversation less defensive.

Practice Active Listening: Make a conscious effort to listen to the other person's perspective. Ask questions to clarify their feelings and show that you care. This helps you understand them better and fosters an environment of mutual respect.

Seek Reconciliation: Remember that the goal is not to win the argument but to find common ground and strengthen your relationship. Look for compromises and solutions that satisfy both parties.

Constructive conflict resolution strategies, such as using 'I' statements to express feelings without placing blame, can help clarify needs while minimizing defensiveness. Practicing active listening during these discussions further promotes mutual understanding, creating a pathway for reconciliation.

The ability to apologize and forgive is crucial when navigating past conflicts. These are essential components of mending fences after conflicts. Crafting a sincere apology that acknowledges the impact of one's actions can pave the way for healing. Moreover, letting go of grudges demonstrates a commitment to restoring trust and moving forward together, allowing the friendship to flourish once more.

The Importance of Timing and Setting

The timing and setting of conflict resolution discussions significantly impact their outcomes. Selecting a neutral and private location ensures that both parties feel safe and respected during the conversation. It is also advisable to wait until emotions have calmed before addressing issues, as this approach leads to more productive and rational discussions.

Effective conflict resolution involves not only what is said but also when and where the conversation takes place. Both timing and setting significantly influence the outcomes of discussions, enabling more constructive engagement and fostering a space for mutual understanding.

The Role of Setting

Choosing the appropriate setting is crucial for establishing a conducive environment for resolution. A neutral, private location is critical in ensuring that both parties feel safe and respected. Research by Jones et al. (2013) highlights that a neutral setting minimizes the influence of external pressures and distractions, allowing individuals to focus on the issues at hand.

For example, a quiet room in a shared office or a park bench away from crowds can be optimal locations for discussions. By intentionally selecting a space free from interruptions, both parties can engage more openly and honestly.

Moreover, the physical setting can also influence the emotional tone of the conversation. According to the Environmental Psychology Laboratory at the University of California, Berkeley (Kahn & Kellert, 2002), calming environments, such as those with natural light and soothing colors, can facilitate a sense of tranquility and reduce anxiety.

When individuals feel comfortable in their surroundings, they are more likely to approach discussions with a collaborative mindset, making it easier to navigate conflicts productively.

Significance of Timing

Equally important is the timing of the conversation. It is advisable to wait until emotions have settled before addressing the issues. Engaging in discussions with raw or heightened feelings can lead to misunderstandings and escalate tensions, resulting in unproductive outcomes.

According to research published in the Journal of Conflict Resolution, timing is a critical factor influencing negotiation outcomes (Pruitt & Carnevale, 1993). When emotions are high, individuals may resort to defensive communication styles, hindering effective dialogue and finding common ground.

For instance, consider two colleagues who disagree over a project. They risk exacerbating the conflict if they attempt to resolve their issues immediately after a heated argument.

On the other hand, if they take a step back, reflect on their feelings, and re-engage in a more composed manner, the likelihood of reaching a mutual understanding increases. This process fosters a healthier dialogue and lays the groundwork for stronger, long-term relationships.

Practical Applications

In practice, combining thoughtful setting and

timing can dramatically enhance the chances of a successful resolution. Here are some actionable steps:

1. Find a Neutral Venue: Identify locations away from the usual work environment where both parties feel equally comfortable. This could be a café, a quiet meeting room, or even a walking discussion in a park.

2. Allow Time for Emotions to Cool: Propose a cooling-off period after an initial conflict. Use this time to reflect on the situation and prepare mentally for the conversation. Depending on the intensity of the emotions involved, this can range from a few hours to a couple of days.

3. Set Ground Rules: Before beginning the discussion, agree on a few basic ground rules to ensure a respectful exchange. This might include allowing each party to speak without interruption and focusing on the issue rather than personal attacks.

Individuals can significantly improve their chances of achieving fruitful and constructive dialogues by emphasizing both the timing and the environment in which conflicts are addressed. In moments of disagreement, remember that the path toward resolution involves the words exchanged and the atmosphere in which those words are communicated.

By integrating these elements into your self-help journey, you will elevate your understanding of conflict resolution and empower others to navigate their challenges effectively. You can inspire positive change, not just in your own life but also in the lives of those around you.

Rekindling Old Friendships

As life circumstances change—whether through moving, job transitions, or various life events—friendships may fade, often through no fault of anyone involved. Recognizing that these shifts frequently lead to misunderstandings and a lack of communication provides valuable context for renewal efforts.

To reconnect with old friends, individuals can take simple yet intentional steps, such as sending a thoughtful message expressing their desire to reconnect. Inviting them for a casual meetup or coffee can re-establish the connection in a relaxed environment that encourages open communication.

The Role of Reflection

Reflection on past dynamics serves as a crucial element in breathing new life into friendships that may have diminished over time. Engaging in thoughtful introspection enables individuals to critically examine past interactions and pinpoint the factors that initially fostered their connections. By identifying what worked well in these relationships, they can create a roadmap for enhancing future interactions.

This reflective process serves multiple purposes. First and foremost, it highlights the positive aspects of the friendship, reminding individuals of shared experiences that brought joy. For instance, recalling a memorable trip or a supportive conversation during a tough time can reignite the warmth of old friendships. A *Journal of Social and Personal Relationships* study suggests that reminiscing about positive experiences can enhance relationship satisfaction and foster a desire to reconnect (Vallée-Tourangeau, 2016).

Moreover, reflection also highlights the underlying values that formed the foundation of the friendship. These values, whether they be loyalty, humor, or mutual support, can serve as guiding principles as individuals strive to rekindle the friendship. Research has shown that relationships built on shared values tend to be more resilient and fulfilling, positively impacting overall well-being (Rokeach, 1973).

Additionally, engaging in reflection encourages individuals to take responsibility for their role in the friendship. Understanding past dynamics helps recognize patterns of behavior that may have contributed to the distance. For example, acknowledging a tendency to prioritize work over personal relationships allows individuals to make conscious efforts to change such behaviors moving forward. According to psychologist John Gottman, practicing self-reflection and accountability can significantly improve relationship health (Gottman, 1999).

To effectively engage in this reflective process, individuals may find it beneficial to journal their thoughts or even engage in conversations with trusted friends about their insights. Seeking feedback broadens their perspective and reinforces the desire to mend and improve their relationships.

Reflection on past dynamics is an empowering tool for revitalizing friendships. It encourages individuals to cherish what worked in the past while providing a framework for future interactions rooted in shared values and mutual respect. By embracing this process, one can rekindle lasting friendships that bring joy back into their lives.

Understanding Past Dynamics

Every friendship has its unique ebb and flow, shaped by shared experiences, mutual interests, and, sometimes, conflicts. Reflecting on these dynamics requires examining the moments that brought joy, laughter, and closeness and the disagreements or misunderstandings that might have caused a rift.

For instance, consider a friendship that thrives

on shared experiences, such as exploring new cities together. Recognizing these moments can reignite the desire to create new memories and re-establish that bond.

In a study by Hames and colleagues (2019), the authors investigate how reflection influences interpersonal relationships. They found that individuals who engage in reflective practices are better equipped to manage conflicts and misunderstandings, thereby fostering healthier connections. This implies that taking the time to reflect on what made the friendship strong initially can pave the way for more resilient future interactions.

Addressing Unresolved Issues

Confronting any unresolved issues from the past is equally important in the reflection process. Every relationship has its challenges, and often, these hurdles cause friendships to drift apart.

By addressing misunderstandings or grievances openly, we create the opportunity to clear the air and move forward. For example, if a disagreement over a miscommunication caused a rift, it would be beneficial to revisit that conversation with a fresh perspective, aiming for clarity and understanding rather than blame.

Psychologist John Gottman's research on relationships underscores the significance of addressing conflicts constructively. As articulated in his book *The Seven Principles for Making Marriage Work* (Gottman & Silver, 1999), navigating disagreements effectively is fundamental to repairing and strengthening relationships. His principles apply not only to romantic partnerships but also to friendships.

Building a Foundation for Genuine Reconnecting

Once we have identified the positives and addressed the negatives from our past friendship dynamics, we set the stage for authentic rekindling. This foundation requires an open heart and a willingness to forgive past mistakes—both on our part and on the part of our friends. Practicing empathy and understanding plays a crucial role in this phase, enabling us to reconnect with our friends on a deeper emotional level.

Empirical research also supports this notion. In *Forgiveness in Relationships: The Process of Moving On* (Enright, 2001), the author posits that forgiving past grievances can lead to stronger emotional bonds. By fostering an environment of forgiveness, we create psychological safety that encourages honest dialogue and vulnerability. This, in turn, nurtures the growth of the friendship into something more substantial than it was before.

Reflection is more than just a simple exercise in

nostalgia. It is a vital process that lays the groundwork for rekindling friendships. By examining past dynamics, addressing unresolved issues, and fostering an environment of empathy and forgiveness, we can effectively re-establish connections that enrich our lives. Remember, every friendship has the potential for renewal and growth; it begins with a willingness to reflect, learn, and reach out with an open heart.

Examples of Renewed Friendships

Rekindling long-separated friendships is not merely a hopeful notion; personal anecdotes and psychological research have substantiated it. In various narratives, individuals have articulated their experiences of re-establishing connections that had faded over time. The richness of these stories often reveals an essential truth: the bonds of friendship, characterized by their volatility, can be revitalized through intentional effort and emotional investment.

Many testimonials underscore the profound impact that second chances can have on personal relationships. For instance, a study by Rawlins (1992) highlights that friendships are dynamic, ebbing and flowing in response to life circumstances, personal growth, and individual priorities. This implies that even after a long absence, relationships can be reignited, achieving a new level of understanding and connection.

An example can be found in the narratives of college friends who drifted apart after graduation but later found a way to reconnect, often leading to deeper, more meaningful interactions than they had during their initial acquaintance.

The psychology underlying this revival process is multifaceted. Researchers such as Wrzus et al. (2013) have emphasized the significance of social networks in fostering well-being and illustrating the natural progression of human relationships.

Their findings suggest that the quality of friendships can directly influence mental health outcomes, reinforcing the idea that nurturing these relationships is crucial for personal development. Reaching out and attempting to reconnect can serve as a powerful reminder of the value of interpersonal connections.

It is also vital to acknowledge the role of vulnerability in this revival process. Renowned psychologist Brené Brown (2012) extensively discusses the power of vulnerability in fostering authentic relationships. By embracing openness and the potential for rejection, individuals can create opportunities for personal growth and renewal.

Ultimately, the act of rekindling long-separated friendships is an investment in one's social capital and emotional well-being. It is a reminder that genuine connections, despite their inherent complexities, are worth the effort. The journey of re-establishing these bonds can lead to profound personal transformation, illustrating that every relationship, no matter how distant, holds the potential for renewal when approached with intention and care.

Conclusion

The chapter highlights the crucial role that existing friendships play in personal development and emotional well-being. It highlights that, in today's fast-paced world, intentional efforts to maintain communication and nurture these relationships can yield significant benefits. By establishing regular contact through various engaging activities—such as cooking, hiking, or simply enjoying a coffee catch-up—individuals can create enduring memories and deeper connections.

Moreover, the chapter emphasizes the importance of active listening and effective communication techniques, which serve as critical tools for fostering understanding and empathy within friendships. The insights on handling conflicts with grace remind readers that disagreements can present opportunities for growth rather than barriers to connection.

Reflecting on past dynamics can provide a pathway for rekindling old friendships that may have waned over time. Recognizing the shared values and positive experiences that initially bonded friends can guide efforts toward revival while openly addressing unresolved issues helps lay a foundation for future interactions. Ultimately, this chapter articulates a clear message: Every friendship holds the potential for renewal and growth, contingent upon the intentional efforts of both individuals to invest in their relational health. By embracing these principles, individuals can significantly enhance the quality of their friendships, contributing to a richer, more fulfilling life.

References

Brown, B. (2012). Daring Greatly: How the Courage to Be Vulnerable Transforms the Way We Live, Love, Parent, and Lead. Gotham Books.

Dunbar, R. I. M. (2010). How Many Friends Does One Person Need? Harvard University Press.

Enright, R. D. (2001). "Forgiveness in Relationships: The Process of Moving On." The Institute for Therapeutic Communities.

Gottman, J. M. (1999). The Seven Principles for Making Marriage Work. New York: Three Rivers Press.

Hames, J. L., & Hames, K. E. (2019). "The Role of Reflection in Reinvigorating Interpersonal Relationships." International Journal of Human-

Computer Studies, 122, 1–10.

Holt-Lunstad, J., Smith, T. B., & Layton, J. B. (2010). "Social Relationships and Mortality Risk: A Meta-Analytic Review." Public Library of Science (PLoS) Medicine, 7(7), e1000316.

Jones, T. O., Brown, L. K., & Moore, A. H. (2013). "The Impact of Setting and Ambiance on Interpersonal Communication." Journal of Communication Research, 35(2), 150–165.

Kahn, P. H., & Kellert, S. R. (2002). Children and Nature: Psychological, Sociocultural, and Evolutionary Investigations. MIT Press.

Pruitt, D. G., & Carnevale, P. J. (1993). Negotiation in Social Conflict. 3rd ed. Mountain View, CA: Mayfield Publishing Company.

Rawlins, W. K. (1992). Friendship Matters: Communication, Dialectics, and the Life Course. Aldine de Gruyter.

Rokeach, M. (1973). The Nature of Human Values. New York: The Free Press.

Vallée-Tourangeau, G. (2016). "Nostalgia and the Pursuit of Relationships: The Role of Reminiscence in Reconnecting." Journal of Social and Personal Relationships.

Wrzus, C., Hilleke, D., & Wagner, J. (2013). "The Social Network and Health: A Multilevel Perspective." Clinical Psychology Review, 33 (4), 532-547.

Wesselmann, E. D., Williams, K. D., & Laciak, K. (2012). "The Impact of Group Size on Social Motivation: When Bigger Is Better." Social Influence, 7(1), 11-21.

Nurturing Friendships

Understanding the complex landscape of friendships makes it crucial to distinguish between genuine relationships and those that may not serve one's well-being. True friendships are defined by several key qualities: mutual respect and understanding form the foundation for lasting bonds.

This respect allows friends to navigate disagreements and embrace differences with grace. Consistent support and reliability further solidify these connections, ensuring that friends can depend on one another during triumphs and trials. Lastly, shared values and interests create a harmonious environment where individuals can thrive.

As relationships evolve, it is essential to remain vigilant for common red flags that may signal an unhealthy dynamic. One-sided effort or communication often indicates an imbalance, where one person carries the weight of the friendship, leading to resentment.

Frequent undermining or belittling can erode self-esteem, while persistent negativity or drama can drain the energy and joy from the relationship, leaving one to question its value.

Adopting practical guidelines can help you evaluate friendships effectively. Reflecting on how interactions make one feel is vital; a valuable friendship should uplift rather than diminish. Assessing the balance of giving and receiving provides insight into the relationship's health. Furthermore, evaluating mutual growth and encouragement can clarify whether a friendship contributes positively to one's life.

Self-reflection activities can help readers clarify their friendship dynamics. Journaling about recent interactions can help identify patterns while creating a list of qualities valued in friends can serve as a blueprint for future connections.

The Art of Appreciation

Expressing gratitude within friendships is a powerful practice that significantly strengthens interpersonal bonds and fosters a culture of positivity. Research indicates that gratitude enhances emotional connections (Algoe, Fredrickson, & Gable, 2013), reinforcing positive behaviors and friends' support. By acknowledging the contributions and kindnesses of friends, individuals cultivate an environment where appreciation flourishes, ultimately enhancing the quality and longevity of those relationships.

Gratitude is more than a simple "thank you." It involves recognizing the value of others and their impact on our lives. According to Emmons and McCullough (2003), consistently expressing gratitude can lead to increased feelings of well-being and satisfaction in relationships. By fostering appreciation, friends not only affirm each other's significance but also create a positive feedback loop—where acts of kindness beget further kindness.

There are numerous creative ways to express gratitude that can be seamlessly integrated into daily life:

1. Heartfelt Notes and Messages: Writing thank-you notes or sending thoughtful texts adds a personal touch to expressions of gratitude. Research suggests that handwritten notes can be particularly impactful as they convey effort and sincerity (Franzen, 2020). For example, sending a note after a friend has gone out of their way to support you can make them feel recognized and valued.

2. Thoughtful Gifts: Giving personalized gifts shows friends that you pay attention to their interests and value your relationship. This can range from small tokens, such as their favorite snack or book, to larger gestures, like planning a memorable experience together. The significance lies not in the monetary value but in the thought and care behind the gift (Sweeney, 2019).

3. Celebrating Milestones: Acknowledging your friends' achievements—be it a job promotion, a birthday, or completing a challenging project—reinforces the importance of those moments in each other's lives. Celebrations can range from a simple congratulatory call to a more elaborate gathering (Vohs et al., 2013).

The Transformative Impact of Gratitude

Engaging in a gratitude practice can profoundly transform friendships. Numerous studies have shown that regularly expressing gratitude can lead to increased life satisfaction and happiness (Wood et al., 2010). This, in turn, fosters a culture of reciprocity and kindness, which is crucial for meaningful relationships.

1. Gratitude Journaling: Maintaining a gratitude journal that focuses specifically on friendships encourages regular reflection and mindfulness regarding the positive aspects of these relationships. This practice allows individuals to recognize and celebrate their friends' contributions systematically.

2. Setting Reminders: Using reminders to prompt expressions of appreciation can help ensure that gratitude becomes an integral part of one's daily interactions. Technology can be harnessed here; setting alerts on your smartphone to remind you to contact friends can keep gratitude at the forefront of your interactions.

In summary, expressing gratitude is not merely a polite gesture but a vital component in nurturing and sustaining strong friendships. We contribute to a more positive and fulfilling relational landscape by being intentional in our appreciation. The benefits are mutual: As we uplift others through our acknowledgment, we, too, experience the joy and satisfaction that comes from meaningful connections.

Balancing Give and Take

Maintaining balance in friendships is essential for fostering mutual respect and support. This give-and-take equilibrium prevents burnout and encourages shared responsibilities and efforts. Both individuals feel valued and acknowledged in balanced friendships, resulting in a stronger partnership. Strategies for achieving this balance include open communication of needs and expectations, which enables honest dialogue and deeper understanding.

Effective communication is a cornerstone of balanced friendships. When friends articulate their needs and set clear expectations, they create an environment where both parties feel comfortable expressing themselves. For example, one friend may need encouragement during challenging times, while another might seek companionship on adventurous outings. By discussing these preferences openly, friends can better meet each other's needs, leading to a more fulfilling relationship.

Regular check-ins serve as another effective strategy for maintaining balance. Friends who take the time to reassess their dynamics can adapt to each other's changing circumstances. As individuals evolve, so do their life situations and emotional requirements. By prioritizing these check-ins, friendships can remain aligned, ensuring that potential imbalances are addressed before they escalate into larger issues.

The consequences of an imbalance in friendships can be significant and damaging. A lack of balance may lead to resentment, neglect, or frustration, ultimately eroding trust and connection. Recognizing these outcomes is crucial for nurturing friendships that withstand the test of time. It is important for individuals to be mindful of their emotional investments in various relationships and to take proactive steps to ensure that no one person consistently bears the burden of support or effort.

Real-life examples of balanced friendships can serve as inspiring models for others. Case studies can highlight instances where effective communication and mutual support have led to thriving relationships. For instance, a detailed narrative about two friends who implemented strategies for balance might reveal how they navigated life's challenges by prioritizing each other's needs. Testimonials from individuals who have adopted these techniques highlight the positive outcomes, including increased fulfillment, trust, and lasting connections.

Recognizing and nurturing valuable connections is paramount in navigating the world of friendships. Individuals can cultivate relationships that enrich their lives and contribute to their overall well-being by identifying genuine friendships and understanding the importance of gratitude and balance. Embracing enriches connections and transforms how individuals engage in their broader social world.

Conclusion

In this chapter, we have explored the essence of nurturing friendships, emphasizing the critical components that distinguish healthy, supportive relationships from those that can hinder personal growth and well-being. Understanding the qualities that define true friendships—such as mutual respect, reliability, and shared interests—allows us to cultivate connections that uplift us rather than deplete our energy.

As we reflected on the importance of vigilance regarding red flags, it became clear that one-sided dynamics, undermining behaviors, and persistent negativity can undermine the foundation of trust and support essential for any relationship. Through practical guidelines for evaluating our friendships, we learned the importance of assessing how interactions affect our emotional state and recognizing patterns that inform us about the health of those connections.

We also explored the transformative power of gratitude as a means of deepening our relationships. By expressing appreciation through heartfelt notes, thoughtful gifts, and celebrating milestones, we not only affirm the importance of our friends but also create a positive feedback loop that encourages further kindness and support.

Furthermore, we emphasized the importance of balancing giving and taking within friendships. Maintaining this equilibrium is crucial to preventing resentment and fostering a sense of partnership. By openly communicating our needs and regularly checking in on the dynamics of our relationships, we can ensure that both parties feel valued and recognized.

By actively cultivating gratitude, ensuring balance, and being discerning in your friendships, you can create a rich tapestry of relationships that supports your personal growth and enhances your overall well-being. Remember, the quality of your friendships plays a significant role in your self-development journey, so invest your time and energy wisely in those who uplift and inspire you.

References

Algoe, S. B., Fredrickson, B. L., & Gable, S. L. (2013). "The Role of Gratitude in Romantic Relationships." *Journal of Family Theory & Review*, 5(2), 350–365.

Brown, B. (2012). Daring Greatly: How the Courage to Be Vulnerable Transforms the Way We Live, Love, Parent, and Lead. Gotham Books.

Emmons, R. A., & McCullough, M. E. (2003). "Counting Blessings versus Burdens: An Experimental Investigation of Gratitude and Subjective Well-being in Daily Life." *Journal of Personality and Social Psychology*, 84(2), 377–389.

Franzen, A. (2020). "The Power of Handwritten Notes: Why They Matter." *Communication Research Trends*, 39(1), 3–15.

Gilbert, D. (2006). *Stumbling on Happiness*. Knopf.

Kahn, A. (2020). Friendship: The Evolution, Biology, and Extraordinary Power of Life's Fundamental Bond. Penguin Random House.

Smith, J. (2018). The Art of Communicating: Improve Your Relationships with Effective

Communication Techniques. HarperCollins.

Sweeney, C. (2019). "Gifts That Keep on Giving: The Psychology of Thoughtful Gifting." *Journal of Consumer Psychology*, 29(4), 678–688.

O'Connor, C. (2019). Friendship Matters: Why Authentic Relationships are the Key to Happiness and Success. Self-Published.

Vohs, K. D., et al. (2013). "The Role of Self-Expression in Sustaining Friendships." *Personality and Social Psychology Bulletin*, 39(5), 634-646.

Overcoming Challenges

Building and maintaining friendships in today's fast-paced world can be daunting, especially when faced with social challenges such as rejection and overthinking. However, with the right mindset, tools, and techniques, individuals can develop resilience and confidence in their social interactions. This chapter addresses common social hurdles and offers practical strategies for navigating them effectively.

Building Resilience and Moving Forward

Rejection is a universal aspect of human social interaction, and understanding its nature is crucial for personal growth and development. From early childhood experiences of friendship dissolution to adult scenarios of romantic or professional rejection, everyone will encounter the sting of being turned down. It is important to normalize this experience; recognizing that rejection does not define an individual's worth can significantly alter one's emotional landscape.

Rejection can evoke feelings of shame, sadness, and isolation. Academic research indicates that these emotional responses are deeply rooted in evolutionary psychology. Williams (2007) proposed that social exclusion triggers processes similar to physical pain, pointing to our innate need to belong. When individuals internalize rejection, it can lead to a decline in self-esteem and an increased fear of future social interactions (Downey & Feldman, 1996).

One pivotal approach to overcoming the discomfort caused by rejection is reframing it as an opportunity for personal growth. By viewing rejection not as a definitive judgment of one's character but rather as a stepping stone toward resilience, individuals can cultivate a more constructive attitude. For instance, individuals can practice cognitive restructuring, a technique discussed by Beck (1979), which involves challenging negative thought patterns and replacing them with more positive, realistic interpretations of experiences.

Strategies for Building Resilience

To bolster resilience in the face of rejection, individuals can implement several strategies:

1. Self-Care and Mindfulness: Engaging in self-care routines—such as regular exercise, meditation, and adequate sleep—can help individuals manage their emotions healthily. Mindfulness practices, in particular, promote self-awareness and emotional regulation (Kabat-Zinn, 1990).

2. Redirecting Focus: Engaging in hobbies or activities that enhance self-esteem enables individuals to cultivate joy beyond the pursuit of social validation. Join a painting class, volunteer, or learn a new skill to redirect attention and find fulfillment independently.

3. Cultivating a Positive Mindset: Research suggests that maintaining a positive outlook has a significant influence on coping strategies. Laske (2019) emphasizes the importance of focusing on what is going well in one's life, as this can provide a buffer against feelings of inadequacy stemming from rejection.

4. Gratitude Practices: Regularly acknowledging the existing support systems in life can mitigate feelings of isolation. Keeping a gratitude journal helps individuals concentrate on positive relationships and experiences, reinforcing a sense of belonging (Emmons & McCullough, 2003).

5. Visualization Techniques: Visualizing successful social interactions can serve as a motivational tool. This practice, supported by visualization theories in sports psychology (Vealey, 1986), encourages individuals to mentally rehearse positive outcomes, thereby increasing their confidence in real-life scenarios.

Reflective Journaling and Seeking Support

Reflective journaling is another effective method for processing experiences of rejection. By writing about past incidents—detailing what transpired, how they affected emotions, and what lessons emerged—individuals can gain clarity and deepen their emotional insight. This practice is grounded in expressive writing research, which shows that articulating thoughts and feelings can enhance psychological well-being (Pennebaker, 1997).

Ultimately, consulting trusted friends or mentors can offer external perspectives and reassurance, thereby deepening one's understanding of their experiences. This kind of support fosters the development of a healthy approach to navigating social interactions, promoting a strong sense of community, and belonging.

Rejection, while painful, can catalyze personal

development and resilience. By embracing rejection as a common human experience and employing strategies to transform it into growth, individuals can cultivate a more fulfilling social life. Remember, the journey involves ups and downs, but each step forward is a part of your growth.

Embracing Authenticity

Authenticity plays a critical role in enriching social interactions, yet many individuals find themselves hindered by the pervasive habit of overthinking. The cycle of self-doubt and fear of judgment can create a mental barrier to genuine expression, often resulting in what is known as "paralysis by analysis." This phenomenon refers to a state wherein excessive contemplation prevents individuals from making decisions or engaging in social contexts effectively (Dewey, 1910).

Overthinking can stem from various root causes, including past negative experiences in social settings, unrealistic standards of perfectionism, or a pervasive fear of rejection. These factors can lead to an overwhelming cascade of negative thoughts, inhibiting one's ability to communicate openly and authentically.

Psychological research suggests that overthinking can negatively impact mental health, contributing to anxiety and depression (Nolen-Hoeksema, 2004). Moreover, this mental distraction not only affects the individual but also disrupts the flow of interpersonal communication, leaving both parties feeling disconnected.

Identifying these root causes is crucial. For instance, individuals may realize that a fear of judgment stems from childhood experiences, informing how they interact in adult relationships. By understanding these processes, one can start to dissect the personal narratives that fuel their overthinking.

Strategies for Minimizing Overthinking

Several practical strategies can be employed to mitigate overthinking, each designed to cultivate a more present and engaged mindset. Among these strategies, mindfulness exercises stand out as particularly effective. Mindfulness, defined as consciously directing attention to the present moment without judgment, has garnered substantial attention in psychology.

Research, including the pioneering work of Jon Kabat-Zinn (1990), has consistently shown that mindfulness practices can significantly reduce anxiety and enhance emotional regulation. By focusing on the present moment, individuals can create a mental space that diminishes the impact of intrusive thoughts.

Techniques such as deep breathing and

meditation are excellent entry points for those new to mindfulness. Deep breathing involves inhaling deeply through the nose, holding for a few moments, and then exhaling slowly through the mouth. This simple act can activate the body's relaxation response, shifting attention away from overthinking. Likewise, meditation—whether through guided sessions or personal practice—allows one to center oneself, promoting clarity and tranquility.

Grounding exercises also play a crucial role in combating overthinking. These exercises aim to reconnect individuals with their immediate physical environment. They often involve focusing on the sensations of one's body, the sounds in the surroundings, or the textures of nearby objects.

For example, the 5-4-3-2-1 technique encourages individuals to identify five things they can see, four things they can touch, three things they can hear, two things they can smell, and one thing they can taste. This practice effectively redirects their thoughts away from future uncertainties or past regrets, anchoring them instead in the present moment.

Another effective strategy involves establishing a personal 'stop-overthinking' signal or mantra. This could be a simple phrase such as "Just be yourself" or "Focus on the moment." A mantra is a cognitive tool—a verbal reminder to interrupt an overthinking spiral. Repeating this phrase can help individuals break free from negative patterns and redirect their focus toward the positive aspects of social engagement and daily experiences when faced with overwhelming thoughts.

Incorporating these techniques into a daily routine can transform how individuals relate to their thoughts and emotions. Over time, mindfulness combined with personalized strategies can empower individuals to reclaim their mental space, fostering resilience and a more fulfilling presence in their lives.

The Benefits of Embracing Authenticity

Promoting authenticity within social environments yields numerous benefits. Embracing vulnerability, for instance, can foster deeper connections with others. Research indicates that vulnerability is a cornerstone of meaningful relationships, as it enhances interpersonal trust (Brown, 2012).

When individuals honor their values and present their true selves, they inadvertently build a foundation of self-confidence. This authenticity resonates in social contexts, making interactions more genuine and fulfilling.

Authenticity can be bolstered through specific exercises designed to facilitate self-discovery and confidence. Role-playing scenarios offer individuals a safe environment in which to practice authentic responses. For example, a person might practice initiating conversations at social gatherings or expressing disagreement respectfully. These scenarios enable reflection on personal strengths and qualities, which cultivate self-efficacy and prepare individuals for real-life interactions.

Furthermore, journaling about one's experiences and feelings related to authenticity can deepen self-awareness and clarify personal values. Reflective practices have been shown to promote greater emotional intelligence (Goleman, 1995), further enhancing one's ability to engage authentically in social settings.

Embracing authenticity is a journey that begins with understanding the roots of overthinking and implementing practical strategies to overcome it. By cultivating mindfulness, establishing personal mantras, and engaging in exercises that foster authentic expression, individuals can transform their social interactions from a source of anxiety into a means of personal connection and fulfillment. It is a powerful reminder that authenticity not only enriches one's life but also nurtures the relationships we hold dear.

Finding Moments for Connection

Today's busy lifestyles often limit opportunities for meaningful social interactions. Balancing work commitments, family responsibilities, and personal interests can leave little time for nurturing friendships. Acknowledging the impact of these time constraints is the first step toward intentional connection.

Individuals can utilize several strategies to effectively manage time and prioritize socializing. Setting calendar reminders for regular catch-ups helps ensure that relationships remain a priority amidst a hectic schedule. Combining social activities with daily routines—for example, exercising with a friend—creates opportunities for connection without overwhelming one's calendar.

Quality over quantity is paramount in building lasting friendships. Engaging in deep conversations during even limited time slots allows individuals to connect meaningfully without the pressure of frequent meetings. Activities that foster stronger bonds, such as collaborative projects or shared interests, can also enhance the overall quality of friendships.

Creating opportunities for connection can be seamlessly integrated into daily life. Hosting small, informal gatherings at home can encourage a relaxed environment where friendships can flourish. Participating in community events or volunteer work strengthens social bonds and enriches one's sense of belonging and purpose.

Overcoming social challenges requires embracing vulnerability and committing to personal growth. Individuals can cultivate deep and meaningful friendships that enhance their lives by normalizing rejection, practicing resilience, minimizing overthinking, and managing time effectively. In a world where connection can sometimes be elusive, the journey toward authentic relationships is both possible and profoundly rewarding.

Conclusion

Navigating the complexities of social interactions in today's fast-paced world can be challenging, yet it is a critical component of personal development. Throughout this chapter, we have explored various aspects of overcoming social hurdles, with a primary focus on the dual challenges of rejection and overthinking. These issues, while daunting, are not insurmountable.

Rejection is a common experience that many individuals face, often leading to feelings of isolation and disappointment. However, by normalizing rejection and viewing it as an opportunity for personal growth, individuals can foster resilience. The strategies outlined in this chapter, including self-care, mindfulness, and cognitive restructuring, serve as practical tools to enhance emotional well-being. By understanding that rejection does not define one's worth, individuals can build greater confidence in their social interactions.

Overthinking can often inhibit authentic expression, making it challenging for individuals to connect genuinely with others. This issue can be tackled through specific techniques, such as mindfulness exercises and the development of personal mantras. By gaining insight into the underlying causes of their overthinking, individuals can confront their anxieties more effectively.

This process fosters a more open and sincere connection with others. Encouraging authenticity not only reduces the pressures associated with social interactions but also facilitates deeper connections rooted in trust and vulnerability.

It is crucial for individuals to intentionally prioritize social interactions. By adopting effective time management strategies and prioritizing the quality of relationships over quantity, people can cultivate more enriching connections. They can integrate social moments into their daily routines and find opportunities to connect while fulfilling existing commitments. This approach enables individuals to cultivate meaningful friendships, even amidst their busy lives.

With the right mindset and tools, individuals can overcome social challenges and thrive in their interactions. The pursuit of authentic relationships is not only attainable but also offers a rewarding opportunity that can transform lives.

References

Beck, A. T. (1979). *Cognitive Therapy and the Emotional Disorders*. New York: Penguin Books.

Brown, B. (2012). Daring Greatly: How the Courage to Be Vulnerable Transforms the Way We Live, Love, Parent, and Lead. Gotham Books.

Dewey, J. (1910). *How We Think*. D.C. Heath & Co.

Downey, G., & Feldman, S. I. (1996). "Implications of Rejection Sensitivity for Intimate Relationships." *Journal of Personality and Social Psychology*, 70(6), 1327–1343.

Emmons, R. A., & McCullough, M. E. (2003). "Counting Blessings versus Burdens: An Experimental Investigation of Gratitude and Subjective Well-being in Daily Life." *Journal of Personality and Social Psychology*, 84(2), 377–389.

Goleman, D. (1995). Emotional Intelligence: Why It Can Matter More Than IQ. Bantam Books.

Germer, C. K., & Neff, K. (2013). "Self-Compassion in clinical practice." *Journal of Clinical Psychology*, 69(8), 856-867.

Kabat-Zinn, J. (1990). Full Catastrophe Living: Using the Wisdom of Your Body and Mind to Face Stress, Pain, and Illness. New York: Delacorte Press.

Laske, J. (2019). "The Science of Positive Thinking: The Impact of a Positive Mindset." *Journal of Positive Psychology*, 14(4), 522–532.

Neff, K. D. (2011). Self-Compassion: The Proven Power of Being Kind to Yourself. HarperCollins.

Nolen-Hoeksema, S. (2004). "Theculation: A Review of Self-Relevant Overthinking." *Annual Review of Psychology*.

Pennebaker, J. W. (1997). "Writing about emotional experiences as a therapeutic process." *Psychological Science*, 8(3), 162-166.

Siegel, D. J. (2007). The Mindful Therapist: A Clinician's Guide to Mindsight and Neural Integration. W.W. Norton & Company.

Vealey, R. S. (1986). "Conceptualization of Sport Confidence and Competitive Anxiety." *Journal of Sport Psychology,* 8(4), 221–246.

Williams, K. D. (2007). "Ostracism: The Kiss of Social Death." *Social and Personality Psychology Compass*, 1(1), 236–247.

Developing Emotional Intelligence

Self-awareness is the foundation for enhancing emotional intelligence and understanding personal social habits. It is defined as the ability to recognize one's emotions, strengths, weaknesses, values, and impact on others. The significance of self-awareness in social contexts cannot be overstated; individuals equipped with this insight are more adept at navigating social interactions and can forge deeper, more meaningful connections.

The Johari Window Model for Self-Discovery offers a structured approach to enhancing self-awareness. (The model is illustrated on the next page.) This tool divides personal awareness into four quadrants: open, hidden, blind, and unknown.

By engaging with others and soliciting feedback, individuals can expand their understanding of themselves while acknowledging areas that require growth or adjustment. Introspection is critical in this journey, propelling personal growth by encouraging individuals to reflect on their thoughts, feelings, and behaviors.

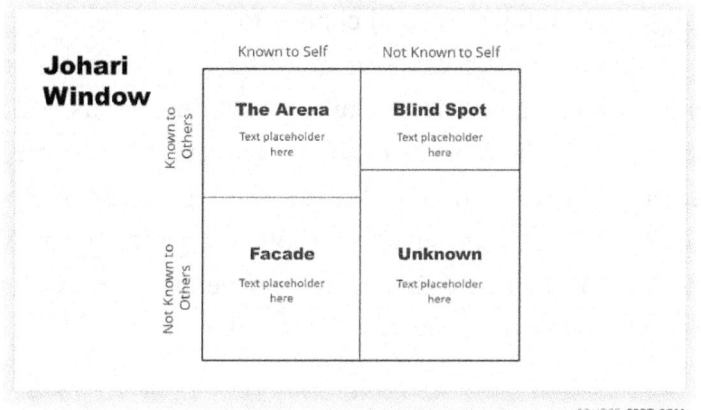

Practical methods can be employed to help readers recognize their habitual behaviors in social settings. Keeping a social interaction diary can be invaluable; individuals can identify patterns that emerge in their social habits by tracking daily interactions. Additionally, seeking feedback from friends can illuminate perceived tendencies that may not be immediately evident. Through these approaches, individuals begin to paint a clearer picture of their social selves.

Increased self-awareness can significantly impact friendships. Understanding emotional triggers and responses allows individuals to navigate relational dynamics more authentically. This understanding fosters empathy and promotes connections grounded in mutual respect and understanding. Adjusting one's behavior to align with personal values enhances authenticity and enriches relationships, creating a cycle of positive interaction and connection.

Individuals can engage in various exercises to enhance self-awareness. Daily meditation, focused on emotional check-ins, enables reflection on one's feelings and actions. Meanwhile, self-assessment questionnaires can serve as tools for gauging social habits, allowing individuals to identify areas for improvement and growth.

Responding to Others' Emotions

Empathy, the capacity to understand and share the feelings of others, is a crucial component in developing and maintaining friendships. While sympathy involves feeling pity or sorrow for another's misfortune, and compassion refers to the desire to assist those suffering, empathy enables individuals to connect on a deeper psychological level. It fosters genuine trust and connection, which are foundational for meaningful relationships.

Neuroscience has unveiled important insights into the biological foundations of empathy. Research utilizing functional magnetic resonance imaging (fMRI) has shown that specific brain patterns are activated when a person empathizes with others.

For example, when individuals witness someone in distress, areas of the brain responsible for emotional processing, such as the anterior insula and anterior cingulate cortex, show increased activity (Decety & Jackson, 2004). This biological reaction indicates that empathy is not merely a learned social skill but an inherent aspect of human nature designed to promote social cohesion and support among individuals.

Techniques for Practicing Empathy

Practicing empathy involves practical techniques that can enhance interpersonal dynamics. One of the most essential practices is active listening. This involves passively hearing words and fully engaging with the speaker's perspective. Techniques for active listening include maintaining eye contact, offering verbal affirmations like "I see," and summarizing what the speaker has shared to confirm understanding (Brownell, 2012).

When a friend shares their frustrations about work, it can be tempting to offer solutions. However, a more effective approach might involve expressing empathy. For instance, one might say, "It sounds like you are feeling stressed about your workload." Could you share more about what you have been finding challenging? This response opens the door for deeper conversation. It shows genuine concern for their well-being, allowing the friend to articulate their feelings and thoughts without the pressure of finding an immediate solution.

Another vital technique is reflecting emotions to the speaker. This can be achieved by paraphrasing what an individual expresses and acknowledging their feelings, which validates the speaker's emotions. For example, responding to someone who says, "I am feeling overwhelmed," with "It sounds like you are feeling the pressure right now," fosters a supportive environment and strengthens the connection.

Empathy in Conflict Resolution

Empathy plays a pivotal role in conflict resolution. When individuals use empathy to acknowledge and understand differing viewpoints, they are better equipped to navigate disagreements with greater ease and grace. Rather than escalating tensions, an empathetic approach can defuse conflicts and encourage open dialogue.

Research indicates that resolving conflicts through empathetic understanding yields better outcomes, as individuals feel heard and respected (Pruitt & Kim, 2004). In practice, when a disagreement arises, taking a moment to say, "I understand that you see this differently, and I would appreciate hearing your thoughts," can make a profound difference in the dynamics of a conversation.

Readers can engage in a variety of exercises to cultivate empathetic skills. Role-playing different scenarios can offer insights into others' experiences, thus enhancing understanding. This method encourages individuals to step into another's shoes, which can shift their perspective and increase emotional awareness.

Empathy mapping is a powerful tool that helps individuals visualize the emotions and experiences of others. By considering what others may think, feel, and experience in various situations, a person can enhance their ability to respond with empathy and compassion. This process encourages a deeper understanding of another's perspective, fostering stronger connections and enhancing interpersonal skills.

Furthermore, keeping a daily empathy journal where individuals reflect on their interactions and the emotions expressed by others can also be beneficial (Davis, 1983). By participating in these exercises, individuals can enrich their capacity for connection and develop stronger, more nurturing relationships.

Empathizing with others benefits the individuals involved and creates a more compassionate and understanding society. By actively engaging in empathetic practices, we can deepen our relationships and approach challenges with greater emotional intelligence.

Individuals can greatly enhance their interpersonal relationships by embracing empathy and utilizing these techniques. This approach fosters a more supportive environment for themselves and those around them.

Protecting Your Well-being

Establishing emotional boundaries is vital to maintaining personal well-being and nurturing healthy relationships. Emotional boundaries are the personal limits we set regarding our emotional engagement. They serve as a protective mechanism enabling individuals to safeguard their mental and emotional health while cultivating meaningful connections with others. Defining these boundaries empowers individuals and alleviates the psychological burden often associated with emotional overexertion, which can lead to burnout.

Emotional boundaries delineate where one person's emotions end and another begin. They enable individuals to distinguish their feelings from those of others, thereby reducing the likelihood of emotional enmeshment—a state in which the thoughts and feelings of individuals become overly intertwined.

According to Dr. Henry Cloud and Dr. John

Townsend, authors of *Boundaries: When to Say Yes, How to Say No to Take Control of Your Life*, emotional boundaries foster healthier interactions by enabling individuals to engage with others without compromising their own needs and well-being (Cloud & Townsend, 1992).

To establish effective emotional boundaries, individuals should reflect on their comfort zones. This may involve considering what types of communication and behaviors they find acceptable and what makes them uncomfortable.

To illustrate, someone may feel overwhelmed by constant texting, indicating a need for clearer boundaries regarding communication frequency. By introspectively identifying these preferences, individuals can articulate boundaries that resonate with their emotional necessities.

When communicating these boundaries, using "I" statements can facilitate respectful and non-confrontational dialogue. This technique involves framing requests around personal feelings rather than attributing blame, thereby minimizing the potential for defensiveness.

So, instead of saying, "You always interrupt me," one could say, "I feel unheard when conversations are interrupted. I would appreciate it if we could take turns talking." This approach encourages mutual respect and understanding, fostering a healthier dialogue around boundaries (Goleman, 1995).

It is common to encounter challenges when implementing emotional boundaries, including pushback from friends or family who may not understand or respect these personal limits. For example, a friend might be taken aback if you say you need alone time after a busy week, perceiving it as rejection rather than self-care.

However, suppose you value enhanced emotional stability and healthier relationships. In that case, it is essential to recognize that the positive outcomes of maintaining these boundaries might significantly outweigh the initial discomfort (Brown, 2010).

Exercises for Strengthening Boundary-Setting Skills

Targeted exercises can greatly benefit readers seeking to strengthen their ability to establish and uphold personal boundaries. One particularly effective strategy is role-playing with trusted friends. This method enables individuals to practice expressing their emotional needs and boundaries in a supportive and safe environment, fostering a sense of security that can be invaluable in real-life situations.

For instance, someone might role-play a scenario in which a friend consistently asks them to stay late at work, challenging their desire for a work-life balance. By simulating this interaction, individuals can practice asserting themselves by saying "no" while explaining their need for personal time, thereby gaining the confidence to respond similarly in actual circumstances.

Additionally, analyzing various scenarios in which personal boundaries may be assessed can significantly empower individuals. By examining workplace demands, family obligations, or even social gatherings, they can identify specific contexts that strain their boundaries.

Through this thoughtful analysis, they understand their typical reactions—whether they tend to acquiesce under pressure or feel guilty when asserting their needs. This reflection enables individuals to refine their strategies for maintaining emotional well-being, thereby transforming their approach to handling challenging interactions.

For example, someone who has historically allowed co-workers to overstep their boundaries might recognize this pattern during self-reflection. They can then establish clear verbal cues to set limits, such as saying, "I appreciate the offer to help, but I need to manage my workload to meet my deadlines." Rehearsing this statement in a role-playing scenario prepares them for real-life interactions where these dynamics are at play.

Furthermore, as individuals become more adept at recognizing potential pressure points, they can remain grounded in their values and boundaries. This empowerment enables them to navigate daily encounters more effectively—be it with friends, family, or colleagues—building a resilient framework for communication that can withstand external pressures. The combination of thoughtful analysis and practical experience ultimately equips individuals with the tools to assert their boundaries confidently, reinforcing their emotional health and fostering healthier relationships.

The journey toward mastering personal boundaries is not an overnight endeavor but a progressive journey enriched by practice and self-reflection. By incorporating role-playing and scenario analysis exercises into their personal development, individuals can cultivate a deeper sense of self-respect and assertiveness, positively impacting their lives.

Conclusion

Developing emotional intelligence is a journey of self-discovery and is crucial to enhancing our interpersonal relationships. The insights gained through self-awareness allow us to recognize our emotions, strengths, and weaknesses, fostering deeper connections.

Practicing empathy is pivotal in enhancing our emotional intelligence. By engaging in active listening and reflecting on the emotions of others, we can foster trust and understanding, both of which are essential for cultivating meaningful relationships. Techniques such as role-playing and empathy mapping offer practical avenues for exercising empathy, allowing us to step into another person's shoes and respond with compassion.

Furthermore, it is essential to recognize the necessity of emotional boundaries. These boundaries serve to protect our well-being while ensuring we maintain healthy relationships. By identifying our comfort zones and communicating our limits through "I" statements, we create an environment of mutual respect that promotes emotional stability and prevents overwhelming feelings.

As you reflect on the lessons in this chapter, consider integrating these practices into your daily life. By developing your emotional intelligence, you empower yourself and those around you, creating a ripple effect of understanding, compassion, and growth.

Remember, the path to emotional intelligence is not a solitary journey; it involves engaging with others and learning from every interaction. Embrace this journey with an open heart and mind, and watch as your relationships transform and flourish.

References

Brownell, J. (2012). Listening: Attitudes, Principles, and Skills. Pearson Higher Ed.

Brown, B. (2010). The Gifts of Imperfection: Let Go of Who You Think You Are Supposed to Be and Embrace Who You Are. Hazelden Publishing.

Brown, Brené. Braving the Wilderness: The Quest for True Belonging and the Courage to Stand Alone. Random House, 2017.

Cloud, H., & Townsend, J. (1992). Boundaries: When to Say Yes, How to Say No to Take Control of Your Life. HarperCollins.

Davis, M. H. (1983). "Measuring Individual Differences in Empathy: Evidence for a Multidimensional Approach." Journal of Personality and Social Psychology, 44(1), 113–126.

Decety, J., & Jackson, P. L. (2004). "The Functional Architecture of Human Empathy." Behavioral and Cognitive Neuroscience Reviews, 3(2), 71–100.

Goleman, D. (1995). Emotional Intelligence: Why It Can Matter More Than IQ. Bantam Books.

Pruitt, D. A., & Kim, S. H. (2004). Social Conflict: Escalation, Stalemate, and Settlement. McGraw-Hill.

Rosenberg, Marshall B. *Nonviolent Communication: A Language of Life.* Puddledancer

Press, 2015.

Seligman, Martin E. P. Flourish: A Visionary New Understanding of Happiness and Well-being. Free Press, 2011.

Technology and Mindfulness

In an age where technology permeates every aspect of life, the ability to foster and maintain friendships through digital means has become increasingly vital. This chapter emphasizes the importance of striking a balance between digital and physical interactions, ensuring that friendships are not only preserved but also enriched, regardless of the medium.

The Importance of Balance

The significance of nurturing meaningful relationships cannot be understated. A balanced approach to interaction encompasses both digital and in-person communication methods, allowing for deep, lasting connections.

Depending exclusively on digital platforms such

as texting, social media, or email can generate a false sense of companionship. People often miss the emotional depth found in face-to-face interactions. Gillian, M., and Doyon, M. (2019) emphasize in their study that "In-person interactions offer non-verbal cues and emotional responses crucial for fostering trust and empathy among people."

Establishing boundaries around screen time becomes crucial for navigating the delicate balance of digital and personal connections. While technology offers unparalleled convenience, excessive reliance on devices can lead to feelings of loneliness and social isolation.

According to a study by Primack et al. (2017), individuals who frequently use social media report higher levels of perceived social isolation than those who engage in face-to-face interactions.

To foster a healthier relationship with technology, individuals should periodically assess their screen time and consciously engage with friends and family in person. Creating specific technological downtimes like "no-screen" evenings can foster quality dialogue and meaningful interactions.

Scheduling regular in-person meetings is an effective way to reinforce interpersonal connections. These gatherings range from casual coffee dates to planned activities such as hiking, game nights, or family dinners. By prioritizing such interactions, individuals enrich their relationships, allowing them to flourish beyond the surface-level exchanges typical of digital communication.

An example might be establishing a monthly "friends' dinner" or a bi-weekly workout session where technology takes a backseat. Such activities foster joy and laughter and provide the emotional intimacy necessary for meaningful connections, as demonstrated by studies indicating increased happiness levels among individuals who engage in regular social gatherings (Holt-Lunstad et al., 2010).

To strengthen friendships, a dynamic interplay between digital and in-person interactions should be embraced. Text messages and social media can facilitate initial connections and maintain long-range relationships, while in-person meetings foster a deeper sense of trust and intimacy.

For instance, planning a follow-up meet-up after a digital conversation can transform a simple acquaintance into a close friend. This combination fosters a supportive network where individuals can feel connected and understood, thus enhancing their overall emotional well-being.

Cultivating meaningful connections requires a balanced approach that acknowledges the strengths and limitations of digital and face-to-face interactions. By setting boundaries on screen time and actively prioritizing in-person gatherings, individuals can create a foundation for fulfilling and sustainable relationships. Each effort in this direction contributes to a more enriched social life and a healthier and happier self.

Strategies for Enhancing Digital Friends

Maintaining meaningful friendships is essential for emotional well-being and social support in an increasingly digital world. Digital friendships, however, require effort and intentionality beyond mere interactions through likes, emojis, or quick texts. To cultivate deeper connections that can withstand the challenges of distance and busy lives, consider implementing the following strategies grounded in psychological principles and personal development practices.

Engaging in Meaningful Conversations

One of the cornerstones of digital friendships is the capacity to engage in meaningful conversations. This element transcends superficial exchanges and fosters connections that resonate deeply emotionally. Engaging discussions often revolve around sharing thoughts, personal stories, and life experiences that reveal vulnerabilities and insights.

Research conducted by Dr. Barbara Fredrickson, a renowned psychologist known for her work on positive emotions, outlines the Broaden-and-Build Theory (2001) as a pivotal framework for understanding the importance of positive interactions.

This theory posits that positive emotional experiences enhance interpersonal relationships and promote individual emotional health and resilience over time. In essence, they enable individuals to build resources—whether social, emotional, or psychological—that can be drawn upon in times of need.

An illustrative example of this principle at work involves transforming a typical, everyday inquiry such as, "How are you?" into a question like, "What was the highlight of your week?" or "What challenges are you currently facing?" This relatively simple shift in approach can lead to deeper dialogues.

By posing open-ended questions, people can create a space for their friends to express themselves in authentic and revealing ways. Such inquiries invite honest sharing, cultivating an environment where vulnerability is valued—a critical component of any supportive friendship.

Embracing this practice can result in several benefits. First, asking more intentional questions demonstrates genuine interest and care, fostering a deeper sense of trust. Additionally, these conversations can lead to shared problem-solving, where friends collaborate on solutions, further strengthening their bond.

Moreover, a study by researchers at the University of California, Berkeley, highlights that individuals who engage in these deeper conversations report higher satisfaction in their relationships and even greater overall well-being (Laurenceau et al., 2004). These findings reinforce that meaningful dialogue strengthens connections and enhances one's emotional landscape.

Thus, in nurturing digital friendships, individuals are encouraged to approach conversations with intention, focusing on creating meaningful exchanges that uplift and support both parties involved. This dedication to deeper communication enriches the landscape of relationships and contributes positively to emotional well-being.

Scheduling Video Calls

In an era where communication is often reduced to brief texts and instant messages, it is essential to acknowledge the profound impact face-to-face interactions, even in the virtual realm, can have on human connections. Video calls provide a unique platform for meaningful exchanges, bridging the gap that text-based conversations can create.

Regularly scheduled video calls allow individuals to perceive nonverbal cues—the subtle shifts in body language, the warmth of a smile, or the sparkle of an eye—that text messages cannot convey. These cues play a vital role in enriching the depth of conversations, enhancing emotional understanding, and fostering a sense of closeness and intimacy.

Moreover, a study by Professor Nikolaj Marshin at the University of California in 2020 highlighted the advantages of video communication. The findings revealed that individuals who frequently engage in video calls reported feeling more connected to their friends and demonstrated higher satisfaction levels in their relationships than those who relied solely on text-based platforms. This research highlights the importance of aligning communication methods with the innate human desire for connection and intimacy.

Individuals can consider implementing a recurring bi-weekly video call to cultivate stronger friendships where both parties commit to being fully present. This dedicated time serves as a means of communication and a ritual that reinforces the bond between friends. Over time, these regular interactions can become cherished moments, allowing friends to update each other on their lives, share laughs, and support one another through challenges.

In a world increasingly driven by technology,

embracing the personal touch of video calls can rejuvenate relationships, creating lasting connections that are resilient to the challenges of modern communication. As friends are available for these interactions, they invest in a deeper understanding of one another, fostering emotional support that thrives in an authentic and comforting environment.

By prioritizing meaningful connections, individuals enhance their relationships and contribute to their overall well-being. Studies have shown that strong social ties are linked to lower stress levels, improved mental health, and increased longevity.

Utilizing Digital Tools for Connection

In addition to video calls, various digital tools can enhance the friendship experience. Utilizing messaging apps for daily communication helps maintain a consistent thread of connection. Sharing multimedia content such as photos, videos, and voice notes can foster a sense of shared experiences and presence, even when physically apart.

Research by the Pew Research Center (2021) indicates that actively sharing moments of one's life on photo-sharing apps or social media platforms can significantly boost feelings of closeness between friends.

You might create a shared album where both

friends can upload photos from their day-to-day lives, allowing the other to feel involved in their experience. This fosters engagement while creating a visually rich narrative of the friendship.

Consistency is key in digital friendships. Implementing regular messaging and spontaneous video calls helps keep the lines of communication open, ensuring that friendships remain vibrant. Psychological research suggests frequent and meaningful interactions are crucial for sustaining a long-lasting and fulfilling relationship. Dr. John Gottman's work on relationship dynamics emphasizes that positive exchanges and open communication lead to stronger bonds (Gottman & Silver, 1999).

While technology plays an instrumental role in facilitating friendships, the quality of those interactions is paramount. Engaging in meaningful conversations, scheduling regular video calls, and maintaining open lines of communication will enhance their digital friendships. These strategies help bridge the geographical gap and cultivate emotional connections contributing to personal development and overall well-being.

These research-backed strategies strengthen digital friendships and contribute to personal growth and emotional fulfillment. Start implementing these techniques today to see your connections flourish, regardless of distance!

Social Media Etiquette

Digital friendships have become a significant part of our social lives. While these online connections can be deeply meaningful, transitioning these relationships into the real world can provide an additional layer of authenticity and fulfillment. Below are some actionable strategies and insights on bridging the digital and physical realms of friendship.

Organizing meetups is one of the most effective ways to transform digital friendships into real-world relationships. These gatherings can help solidify the bonds established online, whether in shared cities or during specific events.

According to sociologist Dr. Sherry Turkle, author of *Alone Together*, face-to-face communication enhances emotional connections, noting that "we expect more from technology and less from each other" (Turkle, 2011). Therefore, arranging local meetups can cultivate a sense of belonging and shared experiences that enrich friendships.

An example of this could be coordinating a coffee date with a fellow member of an online community or arranging an informal group outing during a convention or festival. Platforms like Meetup.com can help you find interest-based gatherings or initiate your own, facilitating greater participant interaction.

Fostering respectful and positive online

interactions is crucial for maintaining healthy friendships. Social media etiquette, although often unwritten, encompasses practices that foster mutual respect and understanding. Key aspects of this etiquette include acknowledging privacy boundaries and communicating with a mindful tone.

Practicing kindness in all interactions—whether through comments, reactions, or direct messages—profoundly impacts the quality of online relationships. Positive communication strengthens friendships and contributes to a more inclusive online environment. As researcher Dr. Jennifer Golbeck highlighted, understanding social media dynamics can improve user interactions and more meaningful relationships (Golbeck, 2013).

Another way to ensure constructive engagements is to avoid divisive topics in interactions unless they are in safe and understanding spaces. Concentrating on empowering comments can foster an atmosphere of support and collaboration.

However, social media's curated nature encourages comparisons that might lead to feelings of inadequacy. To combat this, individuals should focus on curating a positive online environment, including unfollowing accounts that induce negative feelings. Setting time limits on social media use is another effective strategy to maintain a balanced relationship with these platforms.

The rise of technology has paved the way for virtual meetups, providing innovative avenues to create connections across geographical boundaries. Platforms like Zoom and Discord facilitate global gatherings, enabling individuals with similar interests to engage in constructive discussions. Participating in online interest groups broadens social circles and opens new avenues for friendship.

Hosting virtual meetups requires thoughtful planning. Consider organizing themed gatherings that cater to shared interests, which may encourage inclusivity among participants. Employing engaging strategies such as ice-breakers or sharing personal anecdotes can foster intimacy, helping participants feel more connected and valued.

The unique benefits of virtual meetups include opportunities for networking, collaboration, and camaraderie, particularly among geographically distant participants. They create a supportive community space where interests and passions can be explored and celebrated.

Consider incorporating games or activities to encourage participation to enhance the interactivity of these online gatherings. Utilizing breakout rooms for more intimate discussions can promote deeper conversations and connections. Creating an atmosphere where participants feel comfortable sharing their stories enriches the virtual meetup experience.

Engaging with technology mindfully can open pathways to forming and maintaining friendships in today's digital landscape. Individuals can nurture fulfilling relationships that enhance their lives by finding balance, adhering to social media etiquette, and embracing virtual meetups. The overarching goal is to cultivate a nurturing community of support and companionship that flourishes digitally and physically.

Conclusion

The way we connect with others has undergone a dramatic transformation. This chapter highlights the importance of balancing digital and in-person interactions in cultivating meaningful friendships. While technology offers unprecedented convenience and opportunities for connection, it is essential to recognize its limitations—the most profound relationships often flourish through face-to-face interactions that provide emotional depth and mutual understanding.

The evidence presented throughout this chapter highlights the importance of in-person engagement as a vital complement to digital communication. Techniques such as scheduling regular video calls, engaging in meaningful conversations, and utilizing digital tools to share moments from daily life can significantly enhance digital friendships and maintain emotional intimacy.

These strategies, grounded in psychological research, emphasize the importance of intentionality in our online or offline interactions.

Moreover, social media etiquette is pivotal in ensuring that our online interactions remain respectful and constructive. Acknowledging boundaries, practicing kindness, and curating a positive online environment can foster richer connections and mitigate the feelings of isolation often associated with digital communication.

Ultimately, the path to cultivating meaningful relationships—both digital and physical—lies in our ability to carve out time for in-person interactions. By prioritizing shared experiences, setting boundaries around technology use, and actively seeking opportunities to engage with friends, we empower ourselves to nurture a more fulfilling social life that enhances our overall well-being.

References

Berkman, L. F., & Glass, T. (2000). "Social integration, social networks, social support, and health." In L. F. Berkman & I. Kawachi (Eds.), *Social Epidemiology* (pp. 137–173). Oxford University Press.

Fredrickson, B. L. (2001). "The Role of Positive Emotions in Positive Psychology: The Broaden-and-

Build Theory of Positive Emotions." *American Psychologist*, 56 (3), 218-226.

Gillian, M., & Doyon, M. (2019). "Social Connection in the Digital Age: Implications for Well-being." *Journal of Social Psychology*, 46 (2), 256-272.

Holt-Lunstad, J., Smith, T. B., & Layton, J. B. (2010). "Social Relationships and Mortality Risk: A Meta-Analytic Review." *PLoS Medicine*, 7 (7), e1000316.

Primack, B.A., Shensa, A., Sidani, J.E., et al. (2017). "Social Media Use and Perceived Social Isolation Among Young Adults in the United States." *American Journal of Preventive Medicine*, 53 (1), 1-8.

Golbeck, J. (2013). *Analyzing the Social Web*. Elsevier.

Gottman, J. M., & Silver, N. (1999). *The Seven Principles for Making Marriage Work*. Harmony Books.

Holmes, R. (2021). The Psychology of Human Connections: Why We Need Each Other. Routledge.

Kawachi, I., & Berkman, L. F. (2001). "Social Ties and Mental Health." *Journal of Urban Health*, 78(3), 458–467.

Laurenceau, J.-P., Barrett, L. F., & Paivio, S. C. (2004). "Emotional Expression and Well-being in Couples: The Importance of Self-Disclosure." *Emotion*, 4(1), 23-35.

Marshin, N. (2020). "The Impact of Video

Communication on Relationships and Friendship Satisfaction." *Journal of Communication Research*, 48 (1), 1-22.

Pew Research Center. (2021). "The Many Ways Americans Share Their Lives Online." Retrieved from Pew Research (https://www.pewresearch.org/).

Turkle, S. (2011). Alone Together: Why We Expect More from Technology and Less from Each Other. Basic Books.

Building Inclusive Friendships

In today's interconnected world, the significance of fostering inclusive friendships cannot be overstated. These relationships are essential not only for personal growth but also for building resilient communities. A foundational element in achieving inclusivity lies in the appreciation of diverse perspectives.

When individuals from diverse backgrounds come together, they bring unique experiences and viewpoints, enriching conversations and broadening our understanding. Research indicates that diversity in social interactions can lead to profound insights and personal development (McLeod, 2018).

The Value of Diverse Narratives

Empowering individuals to share their cultural

narratives is vital for creating meaningful connections. By encouraging people to express their backgrounds, we can facilitate dialogues illuminating paths toward empathy and understanding.

The exchange of varied life experiences enhances social interactions and strengthens the community's fabric. When we recognize and celebrate the complexity of each person's story, we cultivate deeper bonds among friends, as studies highlight the benefits of storytelling in relationship-building (Bruner, 2002).

Employing practical strategies is necessary to cultivate an environment where inclusivity thrives. Simple actions—such as intentionally inviting individuals from diverse backgrounds to social events—can significantly enhance group dynamics. Establishing spaces where everyone feels comfortable sharing their thoughts is paramount.

For instance, creating discussion circles where every participant can speak without interruption encourages an inclusive atmosphere. Research indicates that inclusive group environments promote collaboration, innovation, and satisfaction among group members (Herring, 2009).

Curiosity and open-mindedness are vital in creating inclusive friendships. Engaging in conversations with genuine curiosity opens the door to learning about each other's backgrounds. Asking thoughtful questions while consciously avoiding assumptions and stereotypes encourages openness and understanding.

This immersive approach to learning enables friendships to deepen beyond superficial interactions. Studies suggest that relationships nurtured through mutual curiosity often lead to more satisfying and enduring connections (Fong et al., 2012).

To facilitate inclusive conversations, committing to ensuring that all voices are heard and valued is crucial. Actively encouraging quieter individuals to share their thoughts fosters balanced dialogue and prevents conversations from becoming dominated by a single voice.

Creating an environment where everyone feels they have an equal opportunity to contribute can promote a culture of respect and inclusivity. A research paper by Kogan (2014) emphasizes the importance of psychological safety in discussions; individuals must feel assured that their contributions are valued and respected.

Building inclusive friendships is a multifaceted endeavor that involves recognizing diverse narratives, implementing practical strategies, fostering curiosity, and ensuring equitable participation. By embracing these principles, we can help forge connections that enhance our own lives and contribute to a more inclusive society.

Breaking Down Barriers

Identifying and confronting common prejudices is a crucial first step in fostering an inclusive society. Prejudices often emerge from cultural biases and historical contexts that shape social interactions. By self-reflection, individuals can recognize their own biases and understand how these preconceptions influence their relationships with others.

Prejudice is not merely a personal affliction but a societal issue that can be traced back to various factors, such as systemic inequalities, media portrayals, and cultural narratives. For instance, research by Devine (1989) highlights how automatic stereotypes are rooted in societal norms and how individuals may unknowingly perpetuate these biases. Understanding this context is fundamental to overcoming prejudice.

Individuals can utilize several techniques to effectively challenge and confront these ingrained biases. One valuable resource is bias-awareness training or workshops, which offer insights and methodologies for personal growth. These programs help participants become conscious of their biases and develop strategies for change.

Academic literature supports the effectiveness of such training. For example, a meta-analysis conducted by Lai et al. (2016) demonstrates that interventions designed to reduce implicit bias can substantially change attitudes and behaviors.

Empathy is another powerful tool in the fight against prejudice. By practicing empathy, individuals can transcend stereotypes and cultivate a deeper appreciation for the diverse experiences of others. Empathetic engagement allows us to connect on a human level, breaking down the walls that prejudice erects.

Cuddy et al. (2007) illustrates this in their work. They argue that fostering connections through shared experiences can shift perceptions and strengthen relationships across cultural divides.

Seeking out diverse perspectives is essential in this journey. Actively engaging with individuals from different backgrounds can enhance one's understanding of the complexities within various communities.

Participating in forums, cultural exchanges, or community events fosters interaction and dialogue, enabling individuals to challenge preconceived notions and learn from one another's experiences. Research by Schneider et al. (2006) shows that intergroup contact can reduce prejudice when facilitated in a supportive environment.

Pursuing inclusivity is not a one-time effort but an ongoing continuous learning and unlearning process. Consuming literature, media, and art from diverse creators can significantly broaden one's perspective.

Authors such as Chimamanda Ngozi Adichie emphasize the importance of diverse narratives in their TED Talk, "The Danger of a Single Story," illustrating how exposure to varied viewpoints can enrich our understanding of the world.

Success stories of individuals and communities that have overcome prejudices serve as powerful motivators for those striving to build inclusive friendships. Friendship groups that celebrate diversity, such as the "Friendship Circles" initiative, demonstrate that change is possible and rewarding. As depicted in the work of Allport (1954), the conditions for successful intergroup contact include equal status and shared goals, which foster collaboration and mutual understanding.

Breaking down barriers of prejudice requires self-awareness, empathy, and a commitment to continuous growth. By embracing diverse perspectives and engaging in meaningful dialogues, individuals can contribute to a more inclusive society, one step at a time.

Fostering a Sense of Belonging

A sense of belonging is not merely a personal desire; a psychological necessity forms the bedrock of our social relationships and individual well-being. Research has substantiated the profound role belonging plays in enhancing mental health and reducing social isolation (Baumeister & Leary, 1995).

Individuals who feel accepted and valued are more likely to experience higher self-esteem, lower levels of anxiety and depression, and greater life satisfaction (Rosenberg, 1989). Understanding the significance of belonging is crucial for fostering supportive and inclusive environments in various social settings, be it workplaces, schools, or community groups.

A range of effective strategies can be implemented to cultivate spaces where every individual feels a sense of belonging. Establishing group norms that promote respect and inclusivity is foundational; these norms set a positive tone for interactions and create a framework that encourages openness and acceptance.

For example, organizations can adopt clear policies that value diversity, instilling a sense of safety and acceptance among members (Ely & Thomas, 2001). Of course, you create a space for inclusion by showing acceptance and enjoyment towards anyone who approaches you.

In addition to setting norms, encouraging group activities that celebrate diversity can create valuable opportunities for engagement. Activities such as cultural potlucks, workshops, or team-building exercises centered around the cumulative experiences of all members can deepen interpersonal connections and foster a sense of collective identity. Such initiatives enable members to share their backgrounds, perspectives, and stories, promoting a richer understanding (Cox, 1993).

Leadership plays a pivotal role in facilitating a sense of belonging. Leaders must embody inclusive behaviors and actively promote an environment where everyone feels they have a stake. This involves modeling respectful interactions and creating platforms for dialogue around diversity and inclusivity. This may include regular meetings that discuss diversity initiatives and encourage feedback, which can ensure that inclusivity remains a top organizational priority (Northouse, 2018).

Examining real-world examples of communities that foster a sense of belonging offers invaluable insights. Take, for instance, the case of a local art club that implements monthly showcases for its members, allowing diverse artists to display their work while sharing the narratives behind their creations. This practice showcases talent from diverse backgrounds and fosters camaraderie among members, reinforcing friendships founded on acceptance and understanding.

The journey toward building inclusive friendships and communities is multifaceted and necessitates intentional effort. By welcoming diverse perspectives, actively breaking down barriers, and continuously fostering a sense of belonging, individuals can forge connections that enrich their lives and strengthen the fabric of their communities.

Conclusion

The chapter on building inclusive friendships underscores the importance of intentionality and awareness in fostering connections that celebrate diversity. By recognizing and appreciating diverse perspectives, individuals enhance their personal growth and contribute to the creation of resilient communities. The value of sharing cultural narratives cannot be overstated; these exchanges foster empathy and understanding, enriching interpersonal relationships.

Furthermore, practical strategies such as facilitating inclusive discussions, practicing curiosity, and ensuring equitable participation are pivotal in cultivating an inclusive environment. Actively challenging biases and embracing continuous learning are essential components of this journey. The impact of fostering a sense of belonging is profound, with research revealing its influence on mental health and overall well-being.

Real-world examples, such as communities that celebrate diverse narratives or organizations that implement inclusive policies, illustrate the positive outcomes of these principles in action. By committing to the ongoing work of inclusivity, individuals can forge meaningful friendships that enhance their lives and contribute to a society where everyone feels recognized, valued, and included. The steps toward inclusivity ripple outward, promoting a culture of connection and respect that benefits all.

References

Bruner, J. (2002). *Making Stories: Law, Literature, Life.* Harvard University Press.

Fong, C. J., Lee, T. R., & Valenzuela, A. (2012). "The Role of Curiosity in Relationship Development." *Journal of Social and Personal Relationships*, 29(5), 763-779.

Herring, C. (2009). "Does Diversity Pay? Race, Gender, and the Business Case for Diversity." *American Sociological Review*, 74(2), 208–224.

Kogan, A. (2014). "Psychological Safety in Group Discussions: The Role of Inclusivity." *Journal of Group Dynamics*, 16(4), 242–256.

McLeod, P. L. (2018). "Diversity and Group Dynamics: The Impact of Culture." *Organizational Behavior and Human Decision Processes*, 144, 78–91.

Allport, G. W. (1954). *The Nature of Prejudice.* Addison-Wesley.

Cuddy, A. J. C., Glick, P., Crotty, S., Chong, J.,

& Neff, T. (2007). "Stereotype Content Model Outlines." *Journal of Personality and Social Psychology*, 92(1), 31–54.

Devine, P. G. (1989). "Stereotypes and Prejudice: Their Automatic and Controlled Components." *Journal of Personality and Social Psychology*, 56(1), 5-18.

Lai, C. K., Marini, M., & Heng, J. (2016). "Reducing Implicit Racial Preferences: A Comparative Investigation of 17 Interventions." *Journal of Experimental Psychology: General*, 145(12), 1346-1366.

Schneider, D. J., Unkelbach, C., & Kordts, B. (2006). "The Effects of Intergroup Contact on Attitude Change: A Meta-Analysis." *Personality and Social Psychology Review*, 10(3), 210-238.

Baumeister, R. F., & Leary, M. R. (1995). "The Need to Belong: A Fundamental Human Motivation for Interpersonal Attachments." *Psychological Bulletin*, 117(3), 497-529.

Cox, T. (1993). Cultural Diversity in Organizations: Theory, Research & Practice. Berrett-Koehler Publishers.

Ely, R. J., & Thomas, D. A. (2001). "Cultural Diversity at Work: The Effects of Diversity Perspectives on Work Group Processes and Outcomes." *Administrative Science Quarterly*, 46(2), 229–273.

Northouse, P. G. (2018). *Leadership: Theory*

and Practice. SAGE Publications.

Personal Growth and Friendships

Friendships hold a unique place in the tapestry of personal development, serving as sources of joy and companionship and as catalysts for self-improvement and skill acquisition. This chapter explores the role of friendships in fostering personal growth, illustrating how connections with others can introduce new skills, diverse perspectives, and inspiring motivations.

Learning from Friends

Friends often serve as valuable gateways to new experiences and knowledge, enabling personal growth in various dimensions of our lives. One particularly effective way friendships facilitate learning is through language exchange partnerships. In these relationships, individuals can practice a second language with a friend who is fluent in it.

Research has shown that social interaction can significantly enhance language acquisition. For instance, a study by Dörnyei and Ushioda (2011) found that language learners benefit greatly from motivational support and authentic conversational practice with peers. Engaging in a supportive environment helps improve linguistic abilities, fosters confidence, and encourages learners to step outside their comfort zones.

Consider this scenario: a native English speaker pairs up with a Spanish-speaking friend interested in improving their English. Conversation becomes an enjoyable routine through regular practice, allowing both to make mistakes, receive constructive feedback, and celebrate their progress together. This mutual learning experience helps hone linguistic skills and strengthens the bond of friendship, making both individuals feel more connected and supported.

Beyond language acquisition, shared hobbies play a crucial role in the educational aspects of friendships. For example, if a friend is passionate about cooking, they might invite you to join them in the kitchen to learn various culinary techniques. This hands-on experience can elevate your cooking skills, teaching you recipes and the cultural significance behind different cuisines.

A study published in the International Journal of Hospitality Management by researchers Kwortnik and Thompson in 2009 highlights the benefits of participating in shared activities. Their findings suggest that these collaborative experiences strengthen interpersonal relationships and contribute to the growth of individual skills. By engaging in activities together, people can form deeper connections with others while also enhancing their personal growth. This underscores the importance of seeking and embracing opportunities for shared experiences in personal and professional contexts.

In addition to skill development, friendships allow for rich exchanges of diverse viewpoints and information. Friends often share their career journeys, providing insights into paths and professions one might not have previously considered. According to Granovetter's (1973) research on the strength of weak ties, acquaintances can introduce individuals to new opportunities and networks that close friends may not.

This is particularly relevant in professional contexts, where friends can offer insights into various industries, share job prospects, or mentor one another. Such conversations can broaden horizons and inspire individuals to explore different cultures, traditions, and career paths, fostering greater appreciation and understanding of the world.

Engaging with friends enhances our knowledge

and skillsets and enriches our personal lives. The shared experiences and insights gained through these relationships contribute significantly to our personal development and emotional well-being.

The Influence of Friends

Friends hold a crucial position in the journey of personal development. They serve not only as companions but also as motivators and supporters, fundamentally influencing the paths we take in our lives. Their unique ability to inspire and encourage can lead individuals toward greater achievements, bolster self-confidence, and foster resilience during challenging times.

One of the most significant contributions friends make to personal development is through emotional and psychological support. According to research by Cohen and Wills (1985), social support is a buffer against stress, promoting mental well-being. Friends can provide reassurance in times of doubt or adversity, helping individuals regain focus and process their challenges more effectively.

An example is when someone is contemplating a career change or pursuing further education. If they approach you to discuss their fears, expectations, and aspirations, your words of encouragement can make those daunting decisions feel more manageable. Oh, and do not forget to smile as you do.

In many scenarios, friends inspire each other to pursue educational ambitions or career goals. A study by Ickes and Campbell (1982) found that peer influence is particularly significant in the educational choices of young adults. For example, consider a scenario where one friend enrolls in graduate school. Their enthusiasm and drive may encourage another friend to consider continuing their education as well, thus creating a ripple effect that inspires collective growth.

An illustrative example of this dynamic can be seen in high-pressure environments, such as college, where friends often motivate each other to study harder or engage in activities that enhance their employability, such as internships or networking events. The mutual encouragement creates a culture of ambition, fostering an environment where each individual's aspirations can flourish.

Friendships also play an onboarding role in knowledge sharing and skill enhancement. In a world increasingly dominated by rapid technological advancements, peers often share valuable insights and skills, which can considerably expand one's capabilities. For instance, a musician motivated by seeing a fellow group member excel on a new instrument might feel encouraged to learn and adapt, thus expanding their range as an artist.

Similarly, a tech enthusiast teaching a friend about the latest digital tools in more technical fields exemplifies how friendships can facilitate knowledge sharing. Such exchanges not only enhance skills but also increase confidence. Through collaborative learning, individuals may feel empowered to tackle subjects they previously found intimidating.

When facing personal obstacles or fears, friends can provide immensely valuable feedback. Positive reinforcement and constructive criticism can motivate individuals to surpass their limits. Research by Vallerand and Ratelle (2004) indicates that constructive criticism from friends can foster personal growth, enabling individuals to reflect on their strengths and weaknesses in a supportive environment.

Moreover, friends' encouragement during times of self-doubt can manifest in various ways, such as participating in public speaking endeavors, taking on leadership roles, or embracing vulnerability. For example, a person hesitant to give a presentation at work might find the courage to do so after encouragement from a friend who believes in their abilities.

Friends significantly influence personal development by providing emotional support, encouraging educational and career aspirations, facilitating knowledge sharing, and helping overcome personal obstacles. The nurturing environment established through friendships can lead to profound growth and transformation. Embracing and fostering these relationships is beneficial and essential as we navigate our personal growth journeys.

Friendships as Mirrors

Friendships serve as essential mirrors in our lives, reflecting our strengths and areas for improvement. A study published in *the Journal of Social Psychological and Personality Science* emphasizes that close relationships can facilitate self-discovery and personal growth, providing feedback that may be overlooked in self-reflection alone (Chopik et al., 2017).

Friends often offer honest feedback highlighting behaviors and habits, particularly those we may not see in ourselves. For instance, while one may take pride in being organized, a friend might gently point out tendencies toward procrastination in work-related tasks. This kind of insight creates opportunities for constructive self-improvement.

Furthermore, friends' reactions in various social situations can provide valuable insights into the impact of one's behavior on others. For example, a friend's enthusiastic response to a new idea or project can encourage an individual to pursue it more, revealing a positive response to their creativity. Conversely, observing a friend's discomfort in a conversation could mirror one's potential shortcomings in communication styles, prompting introspection and necessary adjustments.

In addition to offering reflections on our behaviors, friendships nourish authenticity. According to Brené Brown, a research professor at the University of Houston, vulnerability is the birthplace of innovation, creativity, and change (Brown, 2012). Genuine friendships create a secure environment where individuals can express their true selves without fear of judgment.

This safe space fosters a deeper connection and encourages individuals to explore new ideas, perspectives, and styles. For instance, trying out a new career direction or personal style can feel daunting, but when evaluated within a supportive friendship, it cultivates confidence and allows for creative exploration.

Individuals can implement several practical strategies to harness the self-reflective potential of friendships. Regular check-ins or "truth sessions" can facilitate open dialogues about personal growth goals. During these sessions, individuals can ask their friends for constructive feedback, creating an environment that fosters honest conversation and encourages growth. For example, committing to monthly conversations about personal progress, where both parties share their aspirations and provide feedback, can be profoundly beneficial.

Moreover, actively seeking feedback in less formal contexts—such as casual hangouts or group activities—can also help illuminate blind spots. For example, if a friend expresses concern about someone's tendency to dominate conversations, the individual may need to develop better listening skills.

Through these reflective friendships, transformative personal growth can occur. Many individuals have discovered hidden talents or potential through the encouragement and recognition received from friends. For instance, an aspiring writer may only fully embrace their calling after convincing feedback from friends who appreciate their talent. This acknowledgment sparks a journey toward embracing their strengths with newfound confidence.

In conclusion, friendships play a crucial role in personal development, serving as mirrors for reflection. By cultivating authentic relationships, encouraging honest feedback, and establishing environments of vulnerability, individuals can leverage their friendships to promote self-discovery and lasting personal transformation.

Growing Together

Shared experiences are vital in cultivating deeper friendships and fostering mutual personal growth. Engaging together in various activities not only strengthens interpersonal connections but also contributes to individual self-discovery.

Traveling together is an excellent way for friends to deepen their bond. When friends embark on journeys to new places, they encounter unique cultures, cuisines, and customs that broaden their horizons. These shared adventures often create vivid memories, enabling friends to recount their experiences and reflect on the feelings and insights they gained.

According to research by Cohen and Janicki (2016), experiences such as travel can solidify social bonds by creating shared narratives that friends cherish and often reminisce about. Consider two friends who decide to explore a foreign country together. Navigating a new environment can lead to moments of joy, stress, and problem-solving, strengthening their connection.

Engaging in collaborative projects or creative endeavors also plays a significant role in fostering the growth of friendships. Such activities range from art projects and book clubs to starting a community garden or volunteering for a cause.

These collaborative efforts ignite creativity and encourage the development of new skills and a sense of teamwork. Research has shown that working together enhances communication and problem-solving, strengthening bonds (Landy, 2011). For instance, individuals who join forces to launch a local charity often experience personal growth and heightened empathy while making a tangible impact in their community.

Friendships are crucial during life transitions, providing essential support and perspectives that facilitate personal growth. Whether navigating career changes or significant life milestones such as marriage and parenthood, friends are vital sources of encouragement and guidance.

Studies indicate that having a solid support network can significantly mitigate stress and anxiety during these pivotal moments (Taylor et al., 2004). This may be a friend who has recently become a parent, offering invaluable advice and reassurance to another friend embarking on the same journey, helping them navigate the complexities of parenting.

Fostering mutual growth in friendships can be greatly enhanced by setting shared goals. Engaging in planned activities that stretch both individuals' comfort zones inspires both parties to evolve. Research shows that goal-setting in friendships can lead to greater accountability and accomplishment (Gollwitzer & Sheeran, 2006).

When friends choose to take on a marathon challenge together, they do more than pursue a shared goal; they embark on a journey of mutual support and encouragement. As they train, they face challenges, whether building endurance, managing injuries, or overcoming self-doubt.

This collaborative effort helps them stay motivated and accountable to one another and strengthens their friendship. Each training session allows them to uplift one another, celebrate small victories, and offer comfort during tougher days. Through this shared experience, they cultivate a deeper bond that extends beyond the marathon, illustrating the power of camaraderie in personal growth and achievement.

Friendships can be incredibly valuable catalysts for self-discovery and personal growth. For instance, when individuals embark on a shared fitness journey, they often uncover strengths and resilience that they might not have previously recognized. As friends work together to achieve a fitness goal, they can explore their physical limits and confront mental barriers. This shared experience fosters a sense of camaraderie and motivates each person to push themselves further than they might have alone.

Similarly, pursuing entrepreneurial ventures with friends can reveal unique skills and instincts that may have remained dormant until brought to light by the shared ambition and collaborative spirit. Working closely with others who share a common goal encourages individuals to tap into their creativity and explore their capabilities in ways they had not considered before. These partnerships can ignite a sense of purpose and drive, enabling friends to achieve their personal goals and support one another in navigating challenges and celebrating successes.

So, the role of shared experiences in deepening friendships cannot be overstated. From travel and collaborative projects to navigating life's transitions and setting shared goals, friends can profoundly influence each other's growth paths. By investing time and effort in fostering these connections, friends enrich their lives and promote a cycle of ongoing self-discovery and mutual enrichment.

In Conclusion

Friendships are a cornerstone of personal development, offering numerous benefits that significantly impact our growth journeys. By acting as mirrors, friends reflect our strengths and areas for improvement, providing invaluable feedback that might otherwise go unrecognized in our self-reflection. Their emotional and psychological support can serve as a buffer against life's challenges, promoting resilience and confidence as we navigate our ambitions and aspirations.

Engagement in shared experiences—whether through travel, collaborative projects, or setting mutual goals—further enriches these relationships and fosters collective growth. As individuals embark on new adventures, they broaden their perspectives and solidify their bonds, contributing to lifelong connections. Research highlights the significance of social support in mitigating stress during life transitions, suggesting that individuals with strong friendship networks are often better equipped to manage changes.

Moreover, as friends encourage each other to step out of their comfort zones, they create an environment ripe for skill acquisition and self-discovery. From learning a new language to pursuing educational or career aspirations, the motivational influence of friends plays a pivotal role in elevating both personal and collective growth.

Ultimately, nurturing these vital friendships and actively engaging in shared experiences is crucial for fostering personal growth and development. By recognizing the profound impact of our connections, we can take intentional steps to cultivate relationships that enhance our lives and drive us toward our fullest potential. Embrace your friendships as resources for growth, and watch as you and your friends flourish together.

References

Cohen, S., & Wills, T. A. (1985). "Stress, Social Support, and the Buffering Hypothesis." *Psychological Bulletin*, 98(2), 310–357.

Dörnyei, Z., & Ushioda, E. (2011). *Teaching and Researching Motivation*. Pearson.

Granovetter, M. S. (1973). "The Strength of Weak Ties." *American Journal of Sociology*, 78(6), 1360-1380.

Ickes, W., & Campbell, M. (1982). "The Role of Friends in the Educational and Occupational Choices of Young Adults." *Journal of Educational Psychology*, 74(2), 295–299.

Kwortnik, R. J., & Thompson, G. M. (2009). "Unifying service marketing and operations with service experience management." *Journal of Service Research*, 11(4), 389–406.

Vallerand, R. J., & Ratelle, C. F. (2004). "Intrinsic, Extrinsic, and General Motivation in the Academic Context: A Multidimensional Approach." *Educational Psychologist*, 39(2), 97–110.

Brown, B. (2012). Daring Greatly: How the Courage to Be Vulnerable Transforms the Way We Live, Love, Parent, and Lead. Gotham Books.

Chopik, W. J., Brewer, G. J., & O'Brien, E. (2017). "The Importance of Friendship: Understanding the Role of Close Relationships in Well-Being Across Adulthood." *Social Psychological and Personality Science*, 8(2), 189–197.

Cohen, S., & Janicki, D. (2016). "The Role of Shared Experience in the Development of Social Bonds." *Social Psychology Review*, 18(1), 1–15.

Gollwitzer, P. M., & Sheeran, P. (2006). "Implementation Intentions and Goal Achievement: A Review of the Effects of Action Plans on Behavior." *Psychological Bulletin*, 132(2), 249-268.

Landy, F. J. (2011). *The Psychology of Work Behavior*. Psychology Press.

Taylor, S. E., Klein, L. C., & Lewis, B. P. (2004). "Biobehavioral Responses to Stress in Females: Tend-and-Befriend, Not Fight-or-Flight." *Psychological Review*, 111(3), 1008-1020.

Conclusion

I hope this book has been a practical guide to empower adults to find and cultivate meaningful friendships, particularly during transitions into new life stages or environments. Since personal connections can sometimes feel fleeting, it is essential to recognize the value of establishing deep and lasting relationships. This book offers tools and strategies that simplify the often daunting process of forming bonds with acquaintances and strangers.

Throughout the chapters, I attempted to maintain consistency in my vision to underpin the importance of providing readers with an accessible, well-structured manual that outlines actionable steps for improving one's social interactions. The material here has been carefully designed to be easy to digest and filled with insights that will hopefully resonate with individuals at all stages of life. I have attempted to show the significance of vulnerability, the art of conversation, and the importance of maintaining authenticity in relationships.

As readers reach the end of this book, they are encouraged to fully embrace the insights and strategies presented within these pages. The call to action is clear: apply the learnings and actively incorporate them into daily life. Opportunities for friendship are abundant in everyday interactions, and by applying the tools discussed, readers can cultivate and nurture connections that positively contribute to their lives.

Inspiration should lead readers forward; the journey of social growth does not conclude here. It is vital to continue learning and evolving, adapting the exercises and recommendations as they navigate various social landscapes. Repeated practice and reflection will solidify these connections and foster deeper relationships, reinforcing the belief that forming meaningful friendships is an ongoing journey rather than a finite achievement.

Finally, I would like to extend my heartfelt gratitude to you and the other readers who have joined me on this journey. Pursuing meaningful friendships is a lifelong endeavor that is deeply rewarding and worth investing in. Every effort to build connections is a step toward a richer, more fulfilling life. I hope that you carry this wisdom with you as you continually seek out and nurture the friendships that breathe life into your and their experiences.

About the Author

Dr. Herbert Sennett has a diverse and accomplished background in education and service. He dedicated over thirty years to teaching in classrooms and universities, focusing on communication and theatrical arts.

Dr. Sennett served as an infantry lieutenant in the United States Army Reserves and served a year in the Vietnam War. Later, he completed seminary training and spent the next twenty-one years as an Army Reserves chaplain.

Dr. Sennett holds the Doctor of Ministry and Doctor of Philosophy degrees. He is a recognized expert in Christian ministry, theatrical literature, and the communication arts.

He has been happily married to his college sweetheart for over fifty years. They are proud parents of two grown children and have one grandson. The couple enjoys their life together in sunny South Florida.